Virginia Woolf's *Mrs. Dalloway:*

BOOKMARKED

ROBIN BLACK

New York, NY

Ig Publishing, Inc.
Box 2547
New York, NY 10163
www.igpub.com

ISBN: 978-1-632461-33-9

PRINTED IN THE UNITED STATES OF AMERICA

FIRST EDITION | FIRST PRINTING

For

Gavin & Laurie

and

David & David

with love,

from your kid sister

INTRODUCTION

LONG BEFORE I EVER READ *Mrs. Dalloway*, I idolized and, in a wishful thinking kind of way, identified with Virginia Woolf. It was the early nineteen-eighties and I was at Sarah Lawrence College where Woolf was a regular subject of posters and tote bags and mugs, and sometimes even books that people read, her books, though her identity as an author seemed distinct from this other role she played. She was a feminist icon, and from walls and desks and dishracks she stared out through those prominent, other-worldly eyes of hers, ethereal in her essence, her swanlike neck improbably supporting all of the genius contained behind the stare. I don't remember much talk about her writing, except that *A Room of One's Own*, some hundred pages long, was often condensed from its original length into a short-form rallying cry signifying all that we knew society had long withheld from women. A rallying cry, or a plaint of resigned recognition: *Sigh. A room of one's own. That's what I need.* I'm sure I said such things, though at eighteen, at nineteen, at twenty, it was hardly what I needed most, and in fact, having fallen out in dramatic fashion with my freshman roommate, I had a room of my own from my second semester on.

I had a literal room of my own anyway, and I very much doubt my understanding of the phrase went far beyond that. I was swathed in privilege, a young white woman who had never experienced any economic hardship, generously supported by affluent parents who asked very little of me at that point. The only demands that kept me from being a productive creative sort as opposed to a frustrated creative sort were those generated by my own emotional instabilities, fears, and the deep inhibitions that thwarted my desire to express myself, leaving me in a kind of shut-down limbo for decades—though at the time, of course, I had no idea what was to come. I understood myself very little, and so, along with many others, would mutter about how if only I had a room of my own, I might get something done.

There is great wisdom to Woolf's essay, of course, and isn't her fault that I, and I'm guessing some others, missed the point. I wonder now how many of us had actually read it. I wonder if *I* had actually read it. Because of my Attentional Deficit Disorder (ADD), diagnosed in my forties but very much a factor my whole life, my relationship to reading anything the least bit "difficult" was complicated, and I was a habitual exaggerator. I am certain that the phrase, "Oh, I love Virginia Woolf," passed my lips many times before I had read any of her formal work, though while in college I did read her published journals and letters and the Quentin Bell biography of her. And so, for quite a while, when I said, "Oh, I love Virginia Woolf," I meant *her*; her, as I understood her to be, which was a hodgepodge of her nephew's account of her, her communications to friends and relatives, her journal entries, and, no minor ingredient here, what I needed her to be.

And what I needed her to be was this: a woman raised in a household that valued intellectual achievement above all else, who had a brilliant and difficult father, who suffered from mental illness, and yet, who somehow got the last laugh because the world recognized her as a genius. That I ignored the bit about her killing herself is a tribute to what I could call youthful myopia but which maybe was just my own, having nothing to do with age. Myopia, callousness, and a degree of ruthlessness. I needed hers to be a triumphant story, because I needed to believe that I too could triumph. I needed to ignore that she had killed herself, because I needed that not to be my fate. And, though it took a lot of reconfiguring of reality for me to see myself in Woolf, even *as* Woolf, I did. After all, I too was an emotionally fragile (I didn't quite perceive how ill, at the time) young woman; I too had an unhappy childhood; I too had a brilliant, narcissistic father; and so, it was very possible, that I too would be proved a genius one day. Wasn't it? That was the hope my idolization of her inspired; though I may have that backwards; the hope may have inspired the idolization. Either way, her killing herself wasn't even a footnote to my fantasy.

I was not unpracticed at making such exclusions, ignoring the more difficult side of things. My own father, an alcoholic who suffered from devastating depression (among other things) was committed to a mental health facility for some months when I was eight years old. All I knew was that one day he was gone, that it had something to do with his having been "difficult," and that when we visited him, I felt scared, and I felt ashamed. But then it was over and no one spoke of it again for many, many years. The hospitalization was over, anyway. My father's difficulties never were, but in terms of anything acknowledged, they might as well have been.

Homes that are organized around the needs of an addict, whatever other illnesses may also be in place, are almost magically good at pretending away disturbing experiences, as are children—superficially, at least. The narrative in which I participated was that my father, a professor and civil rights lawyer, was a success, largely because of his fierce intellect; and that his success and that intellect eclipsed all else. We were a perfect family and ours was a happy home.

Denial is a powerful force.

Though it has its limits. Before I reached college to encounter Woolf's face everywhere, I had grown afraid of the ferocity of my own emotions. I was a scared, depressed young woman. My ADD, decades away from being diagnosed, had made schoolwork mysteriously difficult for me, and in my family, academic achievement was the *sine qua non* without which nothing else much mattered. Or anyway, to me, the only family member for whom those achievements were impossible, it seemed that way. I was in a constant dance with D's and C's and the occasional F, and then, out of the blue, the even more occasional A+. The rap on me, as on many people with ADD, was that I was lazy, that I didn't care, that I was comically messy, and that I was willfully tanking my own prospects. In fact, I was frustrated, confused, depressed and dogged by a sense that whatever I did, however I tried, I was likely to fail—for reasons I did not understand.

Between those experiences, and the difficulties associated with my father, I was a wreck. I may not have been fully aware of all the factors that brought me to that point, nor where it was all going, but I was aware enough to be scared of where my own emotions might lead.

The summer I was seventeen, I volunteered with Reading For The Blind, and was assigned work for a psychologist. The article I was to read involved the subject of suicide, though I don't know from exactly what angle. I was too scared to read it, too worried that somehow it would push me over some terrifying edge. One or both of my brothers did the taping for me, while I stayed in another room, cowering.

The fear that I might "do something" reappeared at times, over the years—though, to be clear, it has not been a worry for a very long time. I am now the age at which Woolf took that heavy-pocketed walk into the River Ouse, and I feel great security that I will do no such thing. Whatever the dangers for me when younger, I have been fortunate enough to live in a time when there are good treatments, both therapeutic and pharmaceutical, and equally fortunate to have been able to afford that help, and further fortunate that those resources "worked" for me. Close to forty years of more or less continual therapy, the life-altering ADD diagnosis, plus a couple of absolutely critical medications, have taken me from being someone who at times doubted she could bear more days of struggle, to someone who feels decidedly, gratefully steady—and steadily grateful. I have my low times, as most of us do, but I no longer wake up each morning wondering if I will be okay or will fall apart at some point in the day, and if falling, how far I might fall.

When I actually got around to reading *Mrs. Dalloway*, at the age of forty-two, in graduate school at the MFA Program for Writers at Warren Wilson, I was far from being that very young woman who feared for herself, though not far from struggles with mental illness. But I was in the process of emerging, in the process of getting well, and, for the first time in my life, in the process of working steadily and with some success at something I very much wanted to do.

I no longer had fantasies that required me to rewrite

Woolf's life, thus making her a safe role model. By then I had been working for years with a therapist who helped me understand that the goals of just writing regularly, and trying to learn how to improve, and doing my best whatever the result, would stand me (and my mental health) in better stead. I no longer wanted to be Woolf, because I wanted to be emotionally healthy more than I wanted to be deemed brilliant.

As a result, I could better see the incredible courage it took for Woolf to write a book featuring a suicidal illness that came so close to her own. Courage, and also generosity as it was clear that much of her effort had been toward educating people about the inhumane care available to people suffering from mental illness. I hadn't even been able to read an article on the subject for fear of its impact on me, yet she had done this, created Septimus Smith and endowed him with the tortures she herself endured during her worst moments. That alone blew me away. That alone made this novel matter to me.

This was also a period of my life when I was discovering that I, whose ADD and related glitches had made learning foreign languages impossible, and reading music impossible, and anything involving numbers incomprehensible, had found the language that comes most naturally to me: the language of the craft of fiction. As much as I loved and in some ways needed to write fiction, I loved studying it more, taking it apart, thinking through how stories, novels, paragraphs, sentences, are put together. After a lifetime of not quite understanding what I was meant to learn, much less how I was meant to learn it, I had found a place of comfort and excitement. I was well on my way to becoming a *bona fide* craft nerd, and *Mrs. Dalloway* played a crucial role in that evolution for me.

My relationship with *Mrs. Dalloway* has also given me a Virginia Woolf to admire and at times to question and at times simply to want to understand, far more real than the one I carried around for years, the one I shaped and contorted to be what I needed her to be—not that I have any illusions of being even close to fully understanding her.

Which I might also say about *Mrs. Dalloway*. One of the beauties of this novel is that no matter how much one studies it, it is impossible to master. In fact, the more I immerse myself in it, the less I believe it subject to complete understanding at all. It is a book so reliant on interpretation, so generous in the degree to which it invites a reader's collaboration, that it is something of a moving target, never still—which is perhaps its greatest achievement. Though that has been a challenge as I have worked on this book, through this pandemic time of ours. I have wanted certainty. I have wanted to say with authority (to borrow from Clarissa) *it is this, it is that*, but in fact the more time I think about *Mrs. Dalloway*, the less I feel that saying anything definitive is the best way for me to capture my experience.

And that experience has not been an undilutedly adoring one. I won't say it's a case of familiarity breeding contempt, not at all, but there are aspects of *Mrs. Dalloway* that irritate me, and the more times I read the novel the harder it became to ignore them. I do cringe at some of the histrionic and, to me, unconvincing emotions displayed—and I am not talking about either Septimus or Lucrezia, who have good reason for their highs and lows. There are aspects that disappoint me, as with Woolf's rather shockingly unsympathetic portrayal of Doris Kilman, who surely, surely might have been shown in a less unrelentingly repulsive light, whatever Clarissa's responses to her. It is a rare failure of compassion on Woolf's part. And I am not a huge fan of the Solitary Traveler. (Is anyone? Yes, of course, some reader out there is.) But what important relationship is wholly without flaw or criticism? And this book, my book, is about a relationship, with all the ups and downs such an entity implies—though more ups than downs. It's a book about a good relationship.

I should add, I am not a Woolf scholar and am well aware of that. The world is chock-a-block with Virginia Woolf scholars, many quite stunningly brilliant. They have written with intelligence and insight on the subject of Woolf's psychology, her conscious attempts to weave together symbols, her unconscious incorporation of Freudian dynamics, viewed her through the lenses of Feminist criticism, Marxist criticism, Queer Theory, and much more. Their work is important and fascinating, and every once in a while, while writing this, I have found myself drifting toward these subjects. "What year was Freud's work on the uncanny translated into English?" I texted my sister-in-law, the psychoanalyst—just before I remembered that I am also not a Freud scholar nor, actually, a scholar at all. "Never mind," I then texted. "I don't even want to know."

And so, I avoided reading any critical texts while writing this book. I needed those voices, those modes of reading, out of my head.

I have written here about *Mrs. Dalloway*, not as a theorist of any kind, nor any kind of scholar, nor even a psychologist manqué (you're welcome) but as a fiction reader who is also a fiction writer. As much as possible, I have tried to make this volume be about the words on the pages of Woolf's novel and how I respond to them, what the experience of being me, reading her book has been like—which means, among other things, a reflection of the ADD mind at work, one part "Oooh, look! A shiny object!" and one part the hyperfocus mode that can make it hard to remember to look up from the screen.

As I send this out into the world, I find myself regularly repeating to myself a statement of Woolf's about every reader being the "infallible judge," because I am certain there are things I see in this novel that others will find off-base, and readings I have made that others may find consider just plain wrong. This is a novel about which people feel strongly, to say the least, and the prospect of an army of *Mrs. Dalloway* devotees rising up against me has haunted me a bit. But at the same time, I am excited to have those conversations, and to hear how others have read this revolutionary novel, and to learn why it has been so important to them, as I share why it has mattered so very much to me.

Robin Black

October, 2021

New York, New York

One

HER HAT

"Not the right hat for early morning, was that it?"

—Virginia Woolf, *Mrs. Dalloway*

I USED TO FIND THE opening pages of *Mrs. Dalloway* a bit disorienting. Not so much now, when I have read them dozens of times, but initially they kept me at bay; though it's not Woolf's fault, it's mine.

All readers are different. I struggle with long paragraphs. My Attention Deficit Disorder (ADD) makes this close to inevitable, and it's possible I have some other neurological glitches making it difficult for me to sort through so many lines of text, so close to one another, so undifferentiated by breaks. I am a habitual skimmer, a skipper, much to my shame and indeed to the detriment of my own work when I first started writing fiction; because in a lot of fiction—though not in *Mrs. Dalloway*, as it happens—a high percentage of long paragraphs center around physical descriptions. And so, avid reader though I have been since early childhood, until my forties I had very little experience reading physical descriptions, which in turn led to my writing very few, a fact I needed the help of others to recognize.

Like many who participate in writing workshops, I came in for a lot of scathing commentary in that setting (my work did, I mean, though it often felt more like the former) and one of the most memorable zingers was a classmate saying (*proclaiming!*) that a story of mine felt like nothing more than "two big brains arguing underwater." There was no clue as to what the characters looked like, she said, nor what they were wearing, nor what the room looked like, what the air felt like, what sounds, smells might be jostling in that air. Oh yes, all the others chimed in, I too would have liked to know some of those things.

To be clear, I hadn't done this on purpose, I wasn't making some statement about the essential, barebones nature of human interactions. It just hadn't occurred to me that these elements might enhance a work. I had devoted so little of my own reading energy to absorbing such things–much less appreciating them. I was all about the internal, the psychological, the interpersonal dynamics, and not so much about how the sunlight hit the crystal glass sitting on the windowsill. Though after I realized this about my work, I did go through a period of adopting a half-hearted, quasi-philosophical defense of the practice, trying to stick a flag in the claim that yes, absolutely, my stripped-down writing *was* a recognition of something or other about the essential nature of human interactions, the universality of a fiction that has no actual description in it; because, hey, then couldn't it be about anyone? About any of us?

But that didn't last long. After an appropriately brief period of defending my own deficiencies, I set about learning how to write physical descriptions, until I started to relish doing so. And so now I too write long, chunky paragraphs filled with what I previously did not see. But, as a reader, I still sometimes skim those I encounter—before remembering to go back and actually read them, optimally with a pen in hand, which keeps my flighty attention where it's meant to be.

So much for introductions. That is mine—of me, as a reader. Or anyway, it is a start.

One of the most important aspects of all novels, every short story, is that no work of fiction is ever the same to any two readers. We writers can easily enough forget that. Maybe it's a byproduct of the natural enough desire that everyone love our work. After all, for our fiction to be universally adored, read exactly as we meant it to be read, every reader who picks it up would have to be similar enough to share an identical, positive response. And there's always that illusion, that hope—or anyway there has been that for me. It's why the first online post by a reader about how bored they were by your novel, or how stuck-up they found your beloved protagonist isn't just disheartening, it's a shock, the pinprick to the fantasy of a world filled with fans who will all understand and appreciate what you have done.

But the fact is, every reader is different, and not just in broad ways—*loved, it! hated it!*—but on the line by line level, in their responses to the collection of tiny moments that make up a novel. I'm not sure I ever understood this as clearly as I do now, now that I have spent a year and more trying to understand why *Mrs. Dalloway* feels so important to me, important for me, urgently in some way my own.

My first time through *Mrs. Dalloway* I gave pretty short shrift to the six paragraphs that precede Clarissa's encounter with Hugh Whitbread. They were just too long, too filled with information to which I couldn't connect, and too much like other paragraphs I had spent decades skipping through, which is a shame, but is also water under a distant bridge as I have by now read them enough times for twenty people. Yet at each reading, it is this passage, seven paragraphs in, that first rivets me to the book. To borrow an image favored by Woolf, this is the initial hinge connecting me:

> . . . [Hugh Whitbread's] wife had some internal ailment, nothing serious, which, as an old friend, Clarissa Dalloway would quite understand without requiring him to specify. Ah yes, she did of course; what a nuisance; and felt very sisterly and oddly conscious at the same time of her hat. Not the right hat for the early morning, was that it?

Maybe it wouldn't be such a crucial passage to me if it came on page eighty-nine. It surely wouldn't stand out as clearly, nor do as much to set the terms of the novel. But there it is, just a very few pages in, just as we are figuring out what sort of book this is to be, what is to be asked of us, and what to be given in return. And so much happens in these few lines, both literally and in terms of what is accomplished for the novel. And so much of what happens resonates for me, for the individual, idiosyncratic reader I am. More than resonates, it catches me, claims and pins my wayward attention.

The action here, such as it, involves Clarissa feeling and thinking. She feels sisterly toward Hugh (or possibly toward Hugh and his invalid wife) and is also aware that she feels sisterly. We know she both feels sisterly and aware of doing so, because, while feeling sisterly, she is "at the same time oddly conscious at the same time of her hat." The "oddly" in there 'belongs' to Clarissa, which is writer-speak for the notion that within the rules governing point of view in this book, that "oddly" is not a distant narrator commenting on the peculiarity of Clarissa Dalloway's awareness of her hat, but is a thought of Clarissa's own. Clarissa herself finds it odd that while having this sisterly feeling (which she is aware she is having) she is also thinking about her hat (which she is aware of doing). So, to be clear, there are at least three things that Clarissa is either feeling or thinking (conscious of) all at once. She 1) feels sisterly, 2) is conscious of her hat, 3) is aware that it's odd that this consciousness of her hat has occurred while she is feeling sisterly.

Part of what jumped out at me here is doubtless just that sense of simultaneous yet not obviously connected feelings and thoughts, an echo of my ADD and the way it can make a kaleidoscope of my own awareness. There might well be readers out there who either don't notice this aspect of this moment or who notice it and even relate to it, but don't carry such a complex set of feelings about the whole business of thinking many things at once.

But the subject of wandering thoughts is a loaded one for me. Not that every instance is inevitably painful or damaging. Having spent more than thirty years cooking for my family, I can easily conjure moments of hearing a child share some minor worry from their day, feeling concern, a gust of parental connection, and at the same time, wondering if I saved the document I was working on; wondering if the chicken I plan to serve is still good; thinking of something that occurred a decade earlier, and then finding it odd that I did. Most of the time, in that familial setting, it has been okay to have my thoughts dart around like that.

And in fact some of what I like best about my own work, the fiction I write, comes out as it does because like many people with ADD, my mind works associatively, making and perceiving connections that are unusual, and sometimes creative. Attentional differences aren't all bad.

But then there have been other times, when my failure to concentrate on one thing and only one thing has taken a nasty turn. All those years of not being able to follow lectures, of not being able to stick to projects, of not quite picking up on social cues, have left me alert to any, even the most benign, instances of a split consciousness out in the world, in other people—and apparently in fictional figures too.

But it isn't just the fact of Clarissa's darting thoughts that I respond to here. It is also the nature of them. Woolf cuts the potential sentimentality of Clarissa's sisterly feeling, with a moment of vanity. Lest we think Clarissa is "soft," or the kind of woman so often seen in fiction who experiences undiluted impulses toward nurturing, the intrusion of her worry about her hat, placing a thought about herself in competition with her empathy toward the Whitbreads, signals that Clarissa is not meant to follow that pattern of idealized, fictional women. And I am allergic to idealized characters, really to idealization in any form.

Experience marks us, and my father was an alcoholic, and like most children of an addict, I lived my young life in a household defined by the unauthored lie that is denial. A lot of the years (and years) of therapy I had, centered on untangling the mess left by the disconnect between my own early perceptions that our home was troubled, and the narrative I signed on to, the one in which everything was fine and we were all happy. This dissonance has left me with both an impatience toward false, prettied-up narratives, in life and in fiction, and a lifelong, continually-running scanner looking for signs of a perspective that resonates with my own, looking for something I can recognize as certain—difficult or not. And very often, it is the difficult truths that resonate most for me, as though I am perpetually seeking confirmation of the story behind the denial, the frightening signs of dysfunction that I perceived as a child that were never fully confirmed until I was an adult.

I haven't always known this about myself. As is true of a surprising number of things, I learned about my own drive toward difficult truths, my aesthetic attraction to bad news, when I began to write and publish fiction, a period that coincided with my most productive years of therapy. When my story collection came out, multiple reviewers used phrases like "unsentimental" and "no sugar coating" and even "brutal." (More than one reviewer used the word "brutal.")

My characters are not idealized, not even a tiny bit. Their stories do not generally end well. They can be tough on one another and on themselves. I didn't set out to write notably "unsentimental" fiction but the experience of having the world react to my work that way made me look at the extent to which I dislike and even in some way feel threatened by anything (and anyone) that tries to make a situation, including the rather broad situation of being a human, seem to be easier or simpler than it actually is. And Clarissa's moment of self-consciousness about her appearance, as tiny a moment as it is, registers for me as a meaningful acknowledgment of larger complexities.

And it makes me like Clarissa more, a fact that reminds me of what I see as a flaw underlying every discussion of whether we writers—mostly women writers –should write characters who are likeable. While the fact that Clarissa can't quite hold a moment of sentimentality here makes me like her more—not that I need to like her; I don't read to make friends—I am sure there are readers out there who would like her more were she the sort to press Hugh Whitbread's hand, eyes tear-filled, heart brimming with nothing more complex than a sincere desire to be of help. I know there are such readers, because I have listened to them tell me they just wish my protagonists were a little less . . . flawed. This notion of characters who are somehow inherently likeable is premised on such a weird idea, the possibility that there are universally liked living, breathing people out there, that it seems nonsensical to me right out of the starting gate—even before you get to the inexplicable theory that we are most interested in reading about people whom we like.

For me, my connection to a work of fiction has less to do with the characters, liked or disliked or neither, and more to do with trusting the author, discovering they have some wisdom to share. Every time I read those lines, and experience Woolf chipping a non-idealized characteristic into Clarissa Dalloway, note her recognition that any moment may be a complicated one, I feel myself relax into the narrative: *Yes! Yes, this has the ring of truth. This is an author who knows something about life that I too know. This is an author I can trust not to pretty up the facts, not to give me a set of people in whom I will be unable to believe.*

And something else happens for me at this passage, no matter how many times I read the novel, no matter what preconceptions from all those readings I carry to this page: Clarissa Dalloway springs to life.

Readers speak of characters who "jump off the page" and we writers worry through this phenomenon, debate the question of what produces that much desired effect, appending odd quirks to our characters, unusual hobbies, unique appearances, relatable emotions, or maybe surprising emotions. We relish any sign that a creation of our own has made the leap. In my novel *Life Drawing*, I purposely leave unanswered the question of whether a character has or hasn't committed a certain act, and some of my happiest moments as a writer have passed while listening to readers argue over whether he *really* did or didn't—as though there were a reality beyond the reaches of my keyboard, beyond the horizons of my imagination, in which this worthy though moody fellow Owen makes decisions for himself, takes actions over which I have no control. And it always feels magical when it happens, some force beyond any calculation on the writer's part intervening to endow this imaginary being with breath, with beating heart. It is arguably the headiest feeling a fiction writer can have.

And—as with everything about this pursuit—there is no one answer as to how to achieve the illusion of life, there is only the relationship of each individual reader with each individual text. Each time I read this encounter between

Clarissa and the admirable Hugh, I feel her break free, free of the flat, inky page, free of my awareness that she is a creation of Woolf's, free even of Woolf's agenda for her—which is a necessary liberation, because Woolf's agenda for Clarissa, in the six paragraphs leading to her meeting Hugh, is a mighty one, and is by no means exclusively or even primarily concerned with having Clarissa spring to life. We are given background on her youth, on the all-important past at Bourton, and on the London neighborhood through which she moves, as well as a brief history lesson on England's recent past. As much as we are in Clarissa's thoughts through that stretch, the effect is less that we get to know her than that we get to know things about her.

I don't say this as a negative. Woolf is doing necessary establishment work. And now that I have read these pages (pen in hand, of course) more times than I can count, I am ever more in awe of the extraordinary job she does setting the world of her book aspinning. But it is that world, far more than the character Clarissa Dalloway, that Woolf makes vivid through this stretch. She invites us into the novel by filtering an extraordinary amount of contextual information through Clarissa Dalloway's consciousness.

In addition to what I list above, we also learn that

Clarissa's house is to be the scene of a catered event that night; that she has lived in Westminster for twenty years; that someone named Peter Walsh, whom she knew as a girl of eighteen, is due back in the country from India soon; that she recently had influenza; that it is June; that The Great War, though over, is still a defining force in the world. We are given an evocative description of Big Ben tolling the hour, and then of the entire scene in and around Bond Street on this June day. Of course, it's not all context and back story; we also do learn something of how Clarissa Dalloway thinks about life:

> For Heaven only knows why one loves it so, how one sees it so, making it up, building it round one, tumbling it, creating it every moment afresh; but the veriest frumps, the most dejected of miseries sitting on doorsteps (drink their downfall) do the same; can't be dealt with, she felt positive, by Acts of Parliament for that very reason: they love life. In people's eyes, in the swing, tramp, and trudge. . . in the triumph and the jingle and the strange high singing of some aeroplane overhead was what she loved; life; London; this moment of June.

These glimpses of the depth of Clarissa's musings steer us in the direction of knowing her, but still, prior to her meeting with Hugh, Clarissa's thoughts on life, on her love of life, on the innate love of life felt by even "the veriest of frumps" are both illustrated and also eclipsed by description of this life that she loves. There is a balancing act here for Woolf, between showing us who this woman is, and building the world through which she moves.

The next paragraph tips even more heavily in the direction of conveying information and atmosphere:

> The War was over, except for some one like Mrs. Foxcroft at the Embassy last night eating her heart out because that nice boy was killed and now the old Manor House must go to a cousin; or Lady Bexborough who opened a bazaar, they said, with the telegram in her hand, John, her favourite, killed; but it was over; thank Heaven—over. It was June. The King and Queen were at the Palace. And everywhere, though it was still so early, there was a beating, a stirring of galloping ponies, tapping of cricket bats; Lords, Ascot, Ranelagh and all the rest of it . . .

Again, though these are Clarissa's reflections, though we are in her thoughts, the main work of this paragraph, which continues for some time with descriptions of the world around Clarissa, is to build that world, and fill in with more contextual information. She has a daughter, it seems; she is descended from courtiers; and she is observant, for sure, we do learn that, but it is what she observes that dominates here.

And then, this happens:

> . . . [Hugh Whitbread's] wife had some internal ailment, nothing serious, which, as an old friend, Clarissa Dalloway would quite understand without requiring him to specify. Ah yes, she did of course; what a nuisance; and felt very sisterly and oddly conscious at the same time of her hat. Not the right hat for the early morning, was that it?

Maybe what makes a character jump off the page needn't be so much about some peculiarity, or vivid characteristics, or a memorable appearance. Maybe it can be as simple as a moment in which the character experiences a split-second emotion that serves no purpose beyond illuminating that character's inner life, implying an existence beyond the book and beyond the author's expository needs. There is no usefulness to Clarissa's feelings and thoughts in these lines beyond revealing her. The effect on me is a kind of decluttering that leaves her fully visible for the first time.

And there is some evidence that in feeling Clarissa come into view, I am responding to something more in the text, beyond this fleeting thought of hers. Following her encounter with Hugh, after they have parted, the nature of Clarissa's musings changes, that meeting forming a kind of fulcrum for Woolf at which the balance between world building and character revelation tips a different way. Clarissa's musings are increasingly about Clarissa, as she "finds herself still arguing. . .that she had been right—and she had too—not to marry [Peter Walsh]," though she still can suffer anguish over that. She contemplates the necessary and welcome independence her marriage to Richard Dalloway allows, as well as disclosing that she feels both "very young" and "unspeakably old," and that she does not think herself clever, or accomplished. It is in these passages that the details of her inner life, and some of her habits, are more fully available.

She also contemplates her own mortality in this stretch,

asking herself if it matters that "she must inevitably cease completely" and expounding, in her thoughts, on why it might be something to resent, or how the thought might become "consoling." Perhaps she will survive somehow "in the streets of London, on the ebb and flow of things." Surely, she and Peter Walsh who "lived in each other" might therefore, in some sense, go on.

In this way, over the course of just a few paragraphs, we see the full spectrum of Clarissa's self-consciousness, from a bit of worry about her hat to an awareness of her own mortality. Woolf marches that tiny, seemingly inconsequential moment of concern over an article of clothing all the way to its inevitable end, an elegant treatise on the subject of the human condition: oddly conscious; oddly conscious of her hat; oddly conscious of herself; oddly conscious of her own death. It's a pretty stunning display of wisdom and writing prowess harnessed into one force.

And all of that is no doubt part of why Clarissa springs to life for me there. But there is also something far smaller at work, maybe even a bit petty on my part: the anxiety she experiences over having perhaps chosen the wrong hat.

The wrong hat. How often have I been wearing the

wrong hat or some metaphorical version of it? It isn't far off to say that I am always wearing the wrong hat—arguably another aspect of my ADD, which can include a tendency toward "not quite getting it" when it comes to things like personal presentation. As a child, I often went to school with rats nest snarls in my hair, and as an adolescent, I was hopeless at intuiting what was in and what was "dorky," very often ending up on the wrong side of that line. Nor did this fade with adulthood. Nine months pregnant with my first child, I found myself, massive and ungainly, in a Laura Ashley store on Madison Avenue staffed by *soigne* young women who seemed to have been born with ash blond ponytails held by black velvet bows, praying, praying that somehow, somehow I might pass for presentable; and almost getting away with it—or so I told myself—until I withdrew my wallet from my purse, and a days old roast beef sandwich tumbled out. We reference that moment to this day, the child I was carrying, now in her thirties, and I: *My roast beef sandwich was showing*, we will say when we have been unable to hide how utterly hopeless we are at the whole being pulled-together thing. *My roast beef sandwich was showing, and everybody saw.*

And just as Clarissa experiences with Hugh Whitbread,

with whom she always feels "skimpy," there are people for me around whom this anxiety is keenest, people so well put together they make me feel that I might as well be wearing garbage bags, and ill-fitting ones at that.

So, I am well-primed to be stirred by Clarissa's moment of sartorial insecurity. And while I may not need to like her in order to believe in her, the reality of her fleeting anxiety and its resonance with so many similar moments of my own, is another reason for me to trust the author, trust the reality of this world, and believe in Clarissa Dalloway.

The funny thing though about reading a book over and over, is that all such reactions, all such appreciations are subject to change over time. You pick up nuances you may have missed. You change your mind about characters, you may even change your opinion of the book. As you evolve over time, so the book also evolves—an outgrowth of the degree to which literature is inevitably a collaboration between writer and reader. It is entirely possible that ten readings of *Mrs. Dalloway* from now, I will have a completely different understanding of why something in my response to the book changes with those very few lines. Or maybe that will no longer be true.

It was only after studying this passage intently for this book, trying to understand my responses to it, that I connected Clarissa's fleeting hat anxiety with one of the central worries of the novel: the question of how an individual, given a life that is going to end, aware of that mortality, lives in society.

Mrs. Dalloway is about many things. On the plot level, it's about a woman of some wealth and standing who, on the day leading into a party she is to throw, has reason to muse on her past and on her present-day life. It is also about a veteran of The Great War who suffers from psychotic episodes, presumably as a result of his service, and who takes his own life just as Clarissa Dalloway's party is to start.

At a slightly deeper level, *Mrs. Dalloway* is about British society, and the devastating impact of the War both on the nation as a whole and on individuals. It is about the convention, benefits, and limitations of marriage. It is also about the failures of the medical profession to treat mental illness effectively or humanely. It is about the roles into which women are pressed by societal expectations. And it is about the degree to which romantic and erotic feelings toward members of one's own gender are forcibly, even violently, written out of that society's narrative.

At a deeper level still, the concern that underlies all of these events and observations is the relationship between our individuality, our singular, mortal life, and our connections to others, including familial connections, marital connection, the connection of a shared past, and, crucially, our national connection. On level after level, *Mrs. Dalloway* illuminates and interrogates the conundrum of the individual in society.

And there it is, as Clarissa exchanges those few pleasantries with Hugh. Her "sisterly" feeling—by definition, familial and therefore group-oriented—exists in uncomfortable simultaneity with her self-consciousness about her hat. Or, to reframe that, Clarissa's feeling of connection to others immediately evokes her consciousness of self; that word, *oddly*, echoing a universe of the discomfort in which these two realities must coexist.

It is fitting that Clarissa enacts this tension in Hugh Whitbread's company. Hugh Whitbread, always well-dressed, costumed for his unspecified position at Court, carrying the despatch box, is a clear representative and representation of State, a reminder of the business of the nation; and the business of the nation, recently enough to be still topmost in mind, has been war, the ultimate arena for this dynamic, placing as it does national requirements in conflict with the value of individual lives.

This aspect of war becomes clearest as we meet Septimus Smith, but it is already alluded to in the long paragraph leading into Clarissa's and Hugh's meeting when we hear of Lady Bexborough "who opened a bazaar, they said, with the telegram in her hand, John, her favourite, killed." It's such a striking image of stuffing down the self for the greater good, Lady Bexborough's personal loss, her grief, enclosed in her grip, while she does what is best for the community, performs her civic duty, opens the bazaar. It demonstrates the far-reaching destruction of war, of course, and does so while displaying vividly the conflict between individuality, the fact of being a specific person, and the requirements of societal bonds.

Lady Bexborough's emotional sublimation reappears a bit later on, when Clarissa thinks of her again: "This late age of the world's experience had bred in them all, all men and women, a well of tears. Tears and sorrows; courage and endurance; a perfectly upright and stoical bearing. Think, for example, of the woman she admired most, Lady Bexborough, opening the bazaar."

That second sentence, consisting of a list, takes us on a steady journey through what it can mean to put one's self aside for the nation. First come the "tears and sorrows," which are personal, individual, uninhibited, and true; then the "courage and endurance," states of being that are not natural reactions, but are required coping mechanisms; and then the "upright and stoical bearing," outward-facing, done for others, and in drastic contrast to whatever tears and sorrows one might have privately experienced. The "late age" may have bred in them all a well of tears, but it has also required that the well be redirected underground. In war, the nation requires sacrifice and then also requires the plastering over of the emotions that sacrifice brings on.

With Septimus Warren Smith, this relationship of individual and society is further complicated by his having survived the war but done so destroyed, numbed to pain and to beauty, thinking that "it might be possible that the world itself is without meaning." Having volunteered to fight and perhaps die for his country, an act encouraged by society, he now discovers, in his broken, desolate state, that his obligation to others means that he cannot, should not, end his own life. First, the natural desire of the individual to live is subsumed by the greater good, and then the resulting desire of the individual to die is also understood to be so subsumed.

Clarissa herself has no personal connection to the war. Her husband is too old to have fought, and her only child, young at the time anyway, is a girl. We hear nothing of any nephews or other relatives killed. In a sense, she is as close to an uninvolved witness to the war as anyone then in England could be. But witnesses need not be detached. Clarissa is clearly moved by the war, and though barely even a witness to Septimus's suicide, her reaction could hardly be more emotional when she learns of it at her party, from his doctor's wife:

> Sinking her voice, drawing Mrs. Dalloway into the shelter of a common femininity, a common pride in the illustrious qualities of husbands and their sad tendency to overwork, Lady Bradshaw (poor goose—one didn't dislike her) murmured how, "just as we were starting, my husband was called up on the telephone, a very sad case. A young man (that is what Sir William is telling Mr. Dalloway) had killed himself. He had been in the army." Oh! thought Clarissa, in the middle of my party, here's death, she thought.

The news of this suicide comes just as Lady Bradshaw is pulling Clarissa into a shared societal circle of "common femininity" as well as common wifely perspectives. But this soothing overlay of normalcy and of placid expectation is shattered by the incongruity of death entering so staged and sheltered an event as Clarissa's party. And unlike Lady Bexborough, carrying on with the bazaar while clutching news of her son's death, Clarissa is so overwhelmed by news of a stranger's suicide that she withdraws into solitude:

> She went on, into the little room where the Prime Minister had gone with Lady Bruton. Perhaps there was somebody there. But there was nobody. The chairs still kept the impress of the Prime Minister and Lady Bruton, she turned deferentially, he sitting four-square, authoritatively. They had been talking about India. There was nobody. The party's splendour fell to the floor, so strange it was to come in alone in her finery.
>
> What business had the Bradshaws to talk of death at her party? A young man had killed himself. And they talked of it at her party—the Bradshaws, talked of death. He had killed himself—but how?

> Always her body went through it first, when she was told, suddenly, of an accident; her dress flamed, her body burnt. He had thrown himself from a window. Up had flashed the ground; through him, blundering, bruising, went the rusty spikes. There he lay with a thud, thud, thud in his brain, and then a suffocation of blackness. So she saw it. But why had he done it? And the Bradshaws talked of it at her party!

Here, among the ghostly impressions left by the Prime Minister and Lady Bruton, those pillars of society, emblems of the nation, a battle takes place between Clarissa's fascination (and identification) with the young man's suicide and her dismay as a hostess that such a thing should be brought to her party. These two things are momentarily held in a kind of balance, as though both were breaches of social etiquette, which she has further breached by abandoning her hostessing duties. And Clarissa's focus on how wrong it is that death be mentioned at the gathering, implies, strongly, that on a symbolic level at least, a central function of such gatherings, a central function of society itself, is to push the notion of mortality to the side.[1]

1. This is further explored in the chapter, "Her Lark, His Plunge."

But that objective fails here, if only briefly, as it did not with all those war deaths which were part of an accepted societal order, and for which society bore up, cultivated stoicism, opened bazaars. Septimus's suicide is so great a violation of the social contract, so powerful a statement of ownership over one's own life, that it sets up a kind of chain reaction of shocking behaviors and shattered expectations.

And of course the norm broken here, the one on which Clarissa first focuses, is the party, Clarissa's party, a group gathering in which she plays a singular role: "The party's splendor fell to the floor, so strange it was to be alone in her finery." The news of the suicide causes the party itself to be bared, it's falling splendor evoking nothing so much as a gown. And as it has been unclothed, Clarissa is again focused on being wrongly dressed, overdressed this time, for what the occasion has become: a solitary meditation on the problem of mortality, on the question of what it means to be alive and to know that one will die.

In a novel, a woman worries that she has worn the wrong hat. And it means absolutely nothing more than that she thinks she may have worn the wrong hat. Or maybe that she tends to worry about her appearance. Maybe not even that. Maybe she was in a hurry when she left the house and she chose the wrong hat. Maybe it is a moment of comedy. I myself have probably written scenes in which characters worry about some piece of clothing without it meaning much; much less symbolizing the struggle of the self-consciously mortal being in an interdependent society hell-bent on ignoring death. And for all I know, Woolf intended none of what I see in those few lines, in Clarissa's interrupted empathy, in her self-consciousness about the hat she put on.

The relationship between author, book, and reader is a peculiar one, a creative collaboration between strangers. As an author, I see it this way: I sit here at my computer and imagine a world, characters, situations, and I take those imaginings and trap them in little black squiggles on the page, where they wait for a reader to release them—by reimagining them. My imagination, that of any writer, cannot be transferred intact to the imagination of a reader. The words on the page, these captors of our fancies, are neither stable enough nor sufficiently directive to ensure that. And being an author requires that one let go of the controls.

The first time I read *Mrs. Dalloway* I was a forty-two year old graduate student with still undiagnosed ADD, someone trying to overcome the emotional damage of a rocky childhood, possessed of a million other issues and blessings. I fell in love with a book that seemed to me to be grappling with issues that preoccupy me, and to do so in a way that rewards endless study—but it is impossible to know if the book I love is the book Woolf thought she wrote. Sometimes, to the author, a hat is just a hat.

When I read that moment now, the encounter with Hugh, Clarissa feeling sisterly, Clarissa at the same time oddly conscious of her hat, I know that I do so with a heavy overlay of my own beliefs and impressions and theories. I have lost a kind of innocence, for better and for worse, the words so imbued now with what I see in them that even as Clarissa's mind drifts to her hat I hear an accompanying narrative: *Ah, life! Ah, mortality! Here we all are, together, alone, in this impossible bind. Now what?*

Two

HER LARK, HIS PLUNGE

"IT IS DIFFICULT—PERHAPS IMPOSSIBLE—for a writer to say anything about his own work," wrote Virginia Woolf in her 1928 introduction to the Modern Library Edition of *Mrs. Dalloway*. "All he has to say has been said as fully and as well as he can in the body of the book itself. If he has failed to make his meaning clear there it is scarcely likely that he will succeed in some pages of preface or postscript."

My own version of this, far less eloquent, also less polite (but thankfully silent) is that when I am tired, or just grumpy, and someone asks me what a story of mine is about, I sometimes think, *If I could tell you that, I wouldn't have had to write it.* And then, out loud, I might say something unhelpful like, "Depressed middle-aged people," or, "The indominable human spirit," not because I am trying to be cute, but because I am well aware that to say, "It's about how this new girl isn't accepted by her class at this so-called progressive school, and then one of the kids has a really weird experience with her, involving a ritual, and in the end it is about that kid's parents getting divorced, and the adult narrator pondering that time," is to drive a stake through the story's heart.

In truth, there is no good answer for me to the question, "What is your story about?" because my plots are never inherently interesting, and my fiction lives or dies on nuance, intimation, observation, insight (if I am lucky), metaphors, moods, and, critically, a reader who makes something compelling of all that.

It goes back to that collaboration I spoke of in the last chapter. Every author relies on a reader's imagination to release the author's own imagination from the inky captivity in which it is held to the page, and every author knows that there is a transformative aspect to that release. Writing *is* a communicative art, but it is a particular and peculiar form of communication because we are not simply trying to tell people things. We are trying to present our own insights and imaginings, our urgency and sense of what matters, in a form that makes collaborators of our readers.

And while this collaboration is the most breathtakingly astounding aspect of writing fiction, it is also one of the most challenging. I learned early on that it is no mean trick to strike the right balance between excessive obscurity and hitting people over the head with explanations of symbols, and of meanings, making damn sure a reader gets your point—as you intended.

This is ultimately an issue of trust and of hope. You *trust* that your reader is reading attentively, and you *hope* that you have done a good job with just enough information, just enough mood, just the right language, symbols, metaphors, and more that a reader will make the connections you placed in the work so that it might mean something more, be about something more, than it is possible to convey in a summary. I believe that process and that gulf between what happens in a story and why a story is meaningful, is related to Woolf's view that there is no point trying to explain a novel, which in turn is why I find it so startling that in the same introduction, Woolf goes on to say this:

> Of *Mrs. Dalloway* . . . one can only bring to light at the moment a few scraps, of little importance, or none perhaps; as that in the first version Septimus,

who later is intended to be her double, had no existence; and that Mrs. Dalloway was originally to kill herself, or perhaps merely to die at the end of her party.

Leaving aside that final revelation here and the oddity of its offhand tomato/tomahhto mention of committing suicide or perhaps *merely* dying, I find the bit about Septimus being "intended to be" Clarissa's double surprising and also intriguing, for more than one reason.

First, having told us that it's useless for authors to say anything about their books, she does; not only about the history of her book's evolution, which might make sense in the context of the earlier statement, but about how she *intends* the book to be read. She could easily enough have left out that clause about her intentions, and stuck to the extra-textual facts about what was and wasn't in the book as she rewrote and revised, but she doesn't. She slips in a hint about the book's symbolic structure, whether because she isn't sure all her readers have understood this adequately, or because she feels it's so obvious that she isn't really giving anything away, or for some other reason, I cannot know.

And then I am struck by the peculiarity of that notion:

the double. Though it sounds pretty matter-of-fact (*Oh right! Of course! He's her double.*) as if we should all know what she means, in fact, once I started thinking about it, I realized that I don't. What is a double? What is the purpose of a double? I have been hearing about doubles in fiction for fifty years or so, but I'm not sure I have ever until now been struck by what an undefined concept it is. Do doubles in all works of fiction function the same way? Is this a standard role? What does a double actually accomplish for a book? (Should I be putting doubles in my work? Am I, without knowing it?)

Whatever the answers, if the one thing Virginia Woolf wants me to know about *Mrs. Dalloway* is that Septimus is intended to be Clarissa's double, it seems worth looking at how all of this works.

So, what is a double?

A double is a literary device, and the thing about literary devices is that they are literary. And they are devices. They aren't modeled on anything that actually happens in our lives. They are part of the artifice of fiction, and its truly strange relationship to reality. We don't live in arcs, complete with dramatic *denouements* and tidy resolutions. Things don't ever begin as fictional stories do, nor end—until we do. (And even then, as Clarissa muses, they may well go on.) And we don't have doubles, which means, among other things, that Woolf cannot directly communicate that status to us—unless of course, she chooses to do so in an introduction to the book, three years after first publishing it.

But short of that, she cannot. Whereas, if she puts a man named Richard Dalloway in this novel, and tells us he is Clarissa's husband, we believe her, and there is no debating the point. He is her husband. That part of Richard's identity is very much under Woolf's control. She cannot wholly determine much else about our reactions to him—except at the extremes. If he beats his wife, we will likely find him odious. As he is, we are probably going to find him somewhere in the neighborhood of innocuous to sweet to frustratingly passive to irritatingly inexpressive to politically unrelatable to wonderfully devoted. So much of that response is based on personal experience and biases, and that—among other areas—is where the reader's take on this novel may wobble and stray from Woolf's conceit. An author cannot control how our life histories and emotional tendencies interact with the characters they create. But where Woolf has 100 percent control is over the fact that

Richard is Clarissa's husband.

With a double, there is no such way to directly communicate the relationship, because a double is entirely a creature of the reader's interpretation. Woolf knew this, which is why she used the word "intended." (She wouldn't say that Richard was *intended* to be Clarissa's husband.) A double is a symbolic, rather than actual, relationship. Clarissa's obituary may read that she leaves behind a daughter, Elizabeth Dalloway Titcomb, and was predeceased by a sister, Sylvia Parry, but it will not mention that her double died tragically at his own hand some years before.

So, if they are to be doubles, as Woolf intends, she is going to have to set things up so that with our interpretative minds we make them that.[1] She is going to have to manipulate us into seeing it—which I know has a somewhat distasteful ring to it, that word "manipulate," but all fiction involves manipulation, that is the nature of the form. It is only a problem when the reader is aware of it.

---

1. I have agonized a bit over whether they are doubles or he is merely her double. I feel like there are great (if also potentially tedious) arguments to be had on this point: Is a person always their double's double? Is doubling necessarily reciprocal? But I don't feel that those arguments have a role in this book, and so, for these purposes, I am stipulating that Septimus is Clarissa's double, and she is his. They are doubles.

One way Woolf does this is by never having Clarissa and Septimus intersect. He is not aware of her at all, and she is only aware of him when she learns of his suicide, in the book's final pages. They have no social relationship, and no causal one either. Neither has a direct impact on the other until the very last pages of the book. (I say "direct" because, of course, in a larger social sense we do all have an impact on one another, and this is a book well aware of that fact.) As far as the reader knows, there is no traditional, plot-related reason for Septimus to be in this book called *Mrs. Dalloway*. For this reason, we are pushed to ask ourselves why he is there, and our answer will necessarily shift into the symbolic realm.

As an example of how this process works, let's say I write a story about one woman who lives on Garnet Street and one woman who lives on Walnut Street. If the two are friends, if they grab lunch sometimes, maybe sleep with each other's partners, maybe one burns down the other's house, then a reader doesn't have to wonder why the story contains both women. It's a story about two people whose lives are linked. But, if the women have no such connection, if they are just two women living their lives without any intersection, then a reader will naturally see their connection as more symbolic than actual, and, very likely, will infer a parallel of some kind.

In the case of *Mrs. Dalloway*, that impression of parallelism is gradually but steadily built. Septimus notices the same car—"*the Proime Minister's kyar*"—that Clarissa notices, and that many others notice as well. But Septimus is the first figure, other than Clarissa, for whom Woolf opens up something like a storyline. Even the literal placement of his introduction on the page, the single sentence paragraph for introduction, followed by the repetition of his name, signals importance:

> Septimus Warren Smith, who found himself unable to pass, heard him.
>
> Septimus Warren Smith, aged about thirty, pale-faced, beak-nosed, wearing brown shoes and a shabby overcoat, with hazel eyes which had that look of apprehension in them which makes complete strangers apprehensive too. The world has raised its whip; where will it descend?

His reaction, which displays a peculiar way of looking at things, to say the least, is compelling, as is his wife Lucrezia's worry that people will notice his peculiarity, followed by her thoughts on his having threatened to kill himself.

One job of an author is to signal to readers to what and to whom they should pay attention. In these opening moments, we can't know what roles Septimus and Lucrezia will play in the book, but we are given enough clues, enough to observe and enough to question, that we intuit that there is, literally, a story there. Very quickly, they are placed into a different category from the many other people we encounter in those opening scenes, the Greek Chorus of Bond Street.

In addition, as the book unfolds, Woolf sets up a series of similarities between Clarissa and Septimus that encourage us to see them as versions of one another. Both Clarissa and Septimus are associated early on with musings on death, and on the nature of existence. Each also experiences an odd sensation around the question of visibility. In Clarissa's case:

> She had the oddest sense of being herself invisible; unseen; unknown; there being no more marrying, no more having of children now, but only this astonishing and rather solemn progress with the rest of them, up Bond Street, this being Mrs. Dalloway;

> not even Clarissa any more; this being Mrs. Richard Dalloway.

She feels herself to be disappearing, while Septimus is acutely, inappropriately aware of being seen all too clearly. Here he is as the "royal personage's" car attracts a crowd:

> It is I who am blocking the way, he thought. Was he not being looked at and pointed at; was he not weighted there, rooted to the pavement, for a purpose? But for what purpose?

Both Clarissa and Septimus also carry a noteworthy, keen awareness that their own histories are not dead, but survive vivid in them, and have made them who they are, and in both cases, the relevant history is gender determined. For him, it is the man's crucible of fighting in World War I. For her it is the womanly (for her generation and social stratum) business of choosing a husband. Both of their histories also include an important, intimate relationship with a member of their own sex, followed by a marriage to a member of the other. Both have lost interest in sexual relations, so that the question of being a "disappointment" to their respective spouses hovers over them.

It is clear that Woolf has taken great care to encourage a reader to see the parallel that she intends, and I think she succeeds. But this still leaves open the question of why. It's a question I cannot answer, as her mind is closed to me, but I can share how this parallel functions for me, which may lend some clues.

1. Structure

As someone whose interest in writing fiction grew out of a passion for moments in which nothing happens, I have had to think a lot about the question of narrative momentum. For a long time, I believed that there was a choice between a) producing a plot, and (b) contemplating the human condition, the latter seeming far superior. Fictional events, to me, to many other writers I know, can seem kind of cheap and made up—in part, because they are made up—while observation of a static, tense, or even not so tense situation can seem like an excellent vehicle for displaying one's self-assessed vast wisdom and insight. Having things actually happen in fiction can strike that sort of author (me) as a competing distraction, pulling attention away from the contemplation of the human condition that has drawn them (me) to write so-called literary fiction in the first place. While working on this chapter, I ran across an interview I did with Foyle's Bookshop, back in 2014 when my novel came out, in which I said just that about myself: "I have had to work hard to understand how my ideas about human motivation, and my understanding of human interaction, can be expressed through the creation of (imaginary) human beings—and specifically of plot."

To some of us, plot just doesn't come naturally. But static fiction, the sort in which nothing much happens beyond the author analyzing what already is, rarely interests anyone else as much as it does the author themselves. That isn't an absolute, because there are masters out there who can pull it off; but not many; and not me. Woolf is such a master, but that isn't what she does in this novel.

As for the worry that having a lot happen (Drama! Plot!) can feel contrived, events are only even potentially experienced as a contrivance when they have no basis in the already existing situation of the story or in the characters therein. When characters create plot by taking actions because of their psychological, moral, intellectual, cultural (and more) make-up, and because of the pressures placed on them by a situation or by changes in that situation, the dichotomy between "plot" and "authorial analysis" is collapsed. It is the author's understanding of people that produces the plot. Much as some authors talk about following the dictates of their characters—*they* tell *me* what to do!—that isn't actually a thing. Those dictates, like everything else about a work of fiction, emanate from the author's head.

This may all sound a bit silly, this worry that one's fiction won't adequately showcase one's seriousness and intelligence, but it is a very real concern some writers have, that forging a plot that relies on such things as suspense distracts from their role in a work's creation; that anything other than pure insight and interpretation obscures and even cheapens their contribution. And even if one doesn't worry about it for reasons relating to one's ego, one may just not have the skill.

One approach to this issue has *Mrs. Dalloway* written all over it: Stories and novels can be made up of many pieces and many characters. It is possible to write a novel that both contains a central static aspect *and* displays plot and momentum, through having more than one plot line and through the use of secondary characters.

I have used this approach in short stories often, because I am driven to write about characters who are stuck—in grief, usually. The widow who cannot get past her husband's death; the father who cannot stop reliving the accident that left his daughter blind; the portrait painter who cannot get over the loss of her lover of a quarter century. In all of these stories and many more, I have used the same strategy of introducing a secondary plot into the work, something that has a clear arc, that includes some level of suspense, and has a clear ending, creating enough momentum to act as a counterbalance to the stuck and static qualities of the central character.

That second plot needn't carry the same level of emotional heft as the original one. It rarely has in my work. The widow's story is structured around her daughter's soccer game, with its set beginning, clear conflict, and clear end. The father's story is structured around a trip with his daughter to meet a potential guide dog for her, a discreet occasion that also has its own beginning and end, and its own storyline. The portrait painter's story is structured around sittings for a commission she takes on, a circumstance that provides those same elements.

Those three stories are what's known as "aftermath stories" meaning that the main problem of the story occurred before the story's start, and that there is a persistent sense that story's resolution –or irresolution- relates to the impact of those earlier events.

I have thought a lot about whether or not *Mrs. Dalloway* is an aftermath story—for Clarissa. Against that notion is the fact that she isn't recovering from a specific event, the fallout from which forms the emotional center of the book. On the other hand, the book is structured around a sense that what came before this day created the relevant pressures on her, and plays a critical role in our sense of what matters to her and about her as a character. So I think the term, and the analyses that accompany it, are apt enough to be useful.

Aftermath stories benefit especially from being structured with more than one storyline. With each of those stories of mine (and many more that I've written) the fact of a pre-narrative loss was my conceptual starting point, and it was only later, as I found myself confronted with a story draft about someone mired in their own emotions and memories, a story in which nothing much happened beyond glacial shifts in those emotions, that I complicated the story's structure with a secondary plot that could provide some otherwise undetectable narrative momentum.

A shift in that secondary storyline can also provide the moment in which the static central figure has an emotional response that provides a sense of closure to the work. There is often a meeting up between the central figure's dilemma and some culminating aspect of the secondary storyline.

The addition of that storyline further adds a new and complicating element: the interaction between the two storylines. What will the reader make of that? What connections will they draw? What interpretations will they make? This can open a work dramatically, the back and forth of the reader's associations between these two narratives, creating what I think of as horizontal movement, an element that can be especially welcome when your central character is "stuck" and is not creating much movement in a forward direction.

As I said, this approach has *Mrs. Dalloway* written all over it.

But after all that talk of "secondary storylines," there's a twist. Woolf actually uses three storylines to create the main structure of *Mrs. Dalloway*:

- Clarissa's state of being, her concerns, her fears, her delights based on all the events in her life before this one day: Provides very little current-day story, lots of observation, not much momentum.

- The party, complete with all preparations: Provides temporal structure for the day, complete with the sensation of moving forward, so some momentum.

- Septimus's day of decision, the will he/won't he around his taking his own life: Provides dramatic suspense, narrative tension, and narrative momentum, as well as raising the stakes in the novel.

Despite the flurry of activity around party prep, Clarissa is the point of stillness in the book. She neither embodies nor generates anything like a traditional plot, and our deepening understanding of her is the main change associated with her.

This is not to say she doesn't experience any events, because she does. She isn't sitting still in a room contemplating mortality. She contemplates mortality while buying flowers in the bustling, wounded world; she is hurt by not being invited to a luncheon (and contemplates mortality); her old beau turns up unexpectedly; her daughter's despised companion lurks; her husband expresses—if not in words—his love for her; the Prime Minister attends her party; a woman she loved in her youth turns up, also unexpectedly; she hears of a young man's suicide and has a bit of an emotional (and existential) crisis as she contemplates mortality. It doesn't add up to much narrative momentum, but it's not what I think of as an uneventful day. Things do happen to and around her, they just don't change her or solve a particular issue she is having or even cause her to see things differently. It is the reader's understanding of Clarissa that accounts for the greatest changes associated with her. We know her better by the end. That's all. Tomorrow, she will wake up worrying the same questions (contemplating mortality) and reliving the same memories, with the additional one now of her party the night before. And she may even spare some thoughts for the veteran who took his own life.

This lack of change in her on this particular day is not itself a change. She has spent decades rehearsing and interrogating her decisions back at Bourton. She is sure she made the right decision in not marrying Peter—but cannot quite put the matter to rest. She is poised in a perpetual state of irresolution over that. Nothing throughout the course of the novel changes her views of those long-ago events, as nothing seems to have done over the course of thirty-odd years.

Nor, understandably enough, has she come to any resolution about her feelings toward her own mortality. When she asks herself as she walks along Bond Street if it matters that one must "cease completely," it doesn't seem like either the first or last time. It seems, much like her thoughts on how, yes, her marital choice was right, it was definitely right, like a conversation she has with herself often, if not daily. And will continue to have.

This constancy is also evident in her final dramatic scene when she is shaken by news of a young man's suicide. Woolf makes clear that her response to that shock does not signal a new aspect to her, but is characteristic of the woman we have come to know in the preceding pages: "Always her body went through it first, when she was told, suddenly, of an accident; her dress flamed, her body burnt." And: "Then (she had felt it only this morning) there was the terror; the overwhelming incapacity, one's parents giving it into one's hands, this life, to be lived to the end, to be walked with serenely; there was in the depths of her heart an awful fear."

Woolf stresses continuity with that "always" and then the reference to the fact that Clarissa felt something similar in the morning. Even as her feelings about Septimus's death evolve and seem to evoke in her a new appreciation for life,

I am unconvinced that anything definitional about her has changed. She is handling a bad moment, and reasserting her equilibrium, rather than transforming herself or being transformed:

> She felt glad that he had done it;[2] thrown it away. The clock was striking. The leaden circles dissolved in the air. He made her feel the beauty; made her feel the fun.

She is clearly in a different emotional place from where she was when she first left her party and entered that room, but this is not a scene in which a character is meaningfully changed by a dramatic event. It is a scene in which a dramatic event brings a character back to her true self, complete with known fears, preoccupations, self-interest, coping methods, and the enjoyment of life we have been told has always been hers. Not a change, but reassertion. Not a new part of her, but a more clearly revealed one.

As Peter Walsh might say: *There she is.*

---

2. This troubling and troublesome first clause is addressed later in this chapter.

In workshop settings, there's an infamous, snippy complaint that often arises: *This isn't really a story; it's portraiture*. It's a criticism that comes up so frequently because of that common gap between *what* people want to read and *why* people want to write.

Most people want to read stories in which events unfold and changes occur, while, as I said, many people start writing because they are interested in what makes people tick, and want to explore and share their insights into that. And workshop members can be pretty contemptuous of anything that feels like wallowing in one's own brilliant observational powers without providing any other reason for a reader to turn the pages.

But, to borrow the term if not the tone, I would contend that the parts of this book that are concerned with Clarissa Dalloway are, for the most part, portraiture, as evidenced by the fact that there is no real tension around her, no pressing questions about what will happen to her, no significant plot-related dilemma, and no meaningful change in her through the book. Portraiture. (The difference between me and the complainer in workshop is that I am not being snippy; I am being admiring.)

But portraiture, with its anemic momentum, is not necessarily the same thing as an unstructured narrative.

Clarissa's narrative has a structural spine. It has a marriage of chronology and happenings. The day of the party creates sequencing and timed requirements: flower shopping, resting, mending, dressing, setting up, greeting. This isn't just any day that might unfold willy-nilly. It is an ordered day. The party creates a secondary plot akin to the ones I referenced in my own work, the soccer game, the portrait sittings, and such.

But even with that structure, there is still very little drama, and essentially no suspense. Which is where Septimus Warren Smith comes in.

Soon after we are set on the day of the party, at the very start of the book, the clock ticking toward it, another clock begins to tick: We learn that Septimus Warren Smith whom we have just met has spoken of killing himself.

There's a lot that goes on beneath the surface for readers, and one of the most fascinating processes to me is this business of the clocks that stories set for themselves If I begin to read a story that opens with a boy boarding a bus for a weeklong music camp, and much is made in the opening scene of how it's a week, it's only a week, and the week is to culminate in a concert about which he is both excited and scared, I will naturally expect the story to cover the duration of that week, cover that concert, and not to end after some incident on day four while Danny is still there, moving into day five, still rehearsing for that final event. He has left for camp, and I expect to see him leave to come home—or at least to know that he is about to. He is nervous about a concert, and I expect at the very least to see him walk out on the stage, or I might learn that he won't be performing. I expect something about the concert to be there at or near the end. Like all expectations in fiction, this one can be violated, but it is still an expectation.

Similarly, if one starts a book with the premise that this is the day of The Party, and the clocks are literally chiming the hours, ticking down to The Party (and also down to death, yes, but right now I'm focused on the party) it is likely that a reader will intuit a novel structure that ends with The Party—which is what happens with *Mrs. Dalloway*. Expectation met.

But something else also happens here. After we are already on the clock that is ticking down to Clarissa's party, we meet Septimus Smith, learn of his threatened suicide; and he and that possibility are grandfathered into Clarissa's timeline. Even the first time I read this novel, I assumed that the issue of Septimus either killing himself or turning away from doing so, would be resolved on a schedule that more or less matched the one for Clarissa's party which would more or less match the duration of the book. It's just how most novels work: once a secondary storyline is introduced, it will very likely reach a resolution in some kind of temporal (and paginated) partnership with the central one. (As an aside, this is also one of the more difficult aspects of novel writing, pulling that simultaneity off without it all looking so contrived that the reader sees too clearly the wizard behind the curtain.)

Appropriately, given what is being contemplated and given the state of his thoughts, Septimus's day does not contain the kind of order that Clarissa's does. Doctor's appointments notwithstanding, it is more chaotic and more meandering. She provides the grounded center of the book, and the structured timeline, and he provides the drama. Put them all together, and you have the perfect traditional, untraditional novel.

The word that comes to my mind to describe this interlocking structure is "gorgeous." It is absolutely gorgeous. Like the workings of a particularly sophisticated clock. Speaking of clocks.

2. Encouraging Interpretation (aka Allowing for Chaos)

It takes an act of interpretation for a reader to determine that Septimus is Clarissa's double, and, because a "double" is a purely symbolic entity in a purely symbolic relationship, the interpretive acts cannot not stop there. Without a reader continually drawing connections, determining—or intuiting—what the parallels mean, and grappling with how to put it all together, there is no point to having a double in a novel, and indeed the doubling is essentially over. The reader must understand that these characters are meant to be read in some kind of symbolic relationship for that relationship to exist. This is true, however conscious or not the reader is of that taking place.

Woolf's decision to put Septimus in there, in that role, was a decision to turn over a huge amount of control to her readers' imaginations. While it is true that every reader of every book inevitably reads their own version, Woolf has maximized the role of subjectivity here.

I started by saying that I have no idea what a double is. The fact is, it is something different for every reader.

For me, it all comes down to what is the same about Clarissa and Septimus, and what is different. Or maybe I mean it all starts there.

Clarissa Dalloway and Septimus Warren Smith are of

different sexes and genders. They are of different economic classes, though interestingly not as different as I first carelessly assumed. She is wealthy, but he is not poor. Woolf did not go for the most extreme contrast she might have—perhaps because to have made him genuinely impoverished would have made it unlikely or impossible that he would consult the doctors she wanted brought into the book. In fact, it would have been much harder for their lives to intersect were he poorer than he is—which is itself a bit of social commentary, though not one that is explicit within the novel. But it is also true that, for the most part, Woolf was careful not to make Clarissa and Septimus diametric opposites, whatever differences they have.

Still, Clarissa has intimate connections to people of power and influence, and Septimus does not. His doctor whom he must pay to see, is her party guest whom she has invited to her home. They are also of different generations, which is critically important in Nineteen-twenty-three England in relation the War. He and his generation fought in it, while for the most part hers did not, nor did her gender, though they have all them been altered by the experience to some degree. She is not suffering from severe mental illness, and he is, though again, we are not talking about simple contrasts, as she is also not exactly a paragon of emotional health. Woolf also makes Clarissa a flu survivor, weakened by her recent bout, so if one broadens the category from mental health to health, there is again an area overlap. And of course, he kills himself, and she does not, and this is, at least for this one day in June, a true and meaningful difference, though in the very long run, since the only choice is suicide or "merely dying" there is some eternal overlap.

A lot can be made of all of these differences, especially given that the two characters are intended to be "doubles," but I do not think Woolf's main goal is to stress the simple or glaring contrasts between Clarissa and Septimus. My experience as a reader is that their similarities and differences, in combination, set Clarissa and Septimus into something like a metaphoric relationship, a pairing in which the interaction between what the two entities have in common and what distinguishes them results in a transformation of my understanding of both.

Here is a simple metaphor: *The stove spewed clouds of black soot, a malevolent dragon in our kitchen.* Through this metaphor, the stove is endowed with the dragon's qualities: with wanting to do harm, with a personality, with will, with volition. The stove, which perhaps had no such quality before, is now tinged with evil. In anything remotely like realist fiction, it is still a stove, any reader knows that it's still a stove and hasn't literally turned into a dragon, but it now has dragonlike aspects to it.

The degree of that, however, is variable among people who read the sentence. The precise way in which anyone interprets this metaphor, the impact it has on how they envision or feel about the stove, is one of those areas over which an author has very limited control. For some, it might be the key to grasping the mood of the scene in which the sentence occurs, for others it may seem a bit clunky, and still other readers might not register it at all.

There is a functional difference between saying "The stove spewed clouds of black soot" and saying "The stove spewed clouds of black soot, a malevolent dragon in our kitchen." This functional difference mimics the difference between asserting that Richard Dalloway is Clarissa's husband, and intending a reader to understand through an act of interpretation that Septimus is Clarissa's double. The author can assert that there is smoke coming out of the stove, and if all they want to do is convey that fact, then mission accomplished. No one can challenge the assertion. But once you have placed a dragon into the reader's imagination, all bets are off.

Metaphors only work at all because of a synthesis of similarity and difference. *The stove spewed clouds of black soot, a frog in our kitchen* is essentially meaningless because there isn't enough of a similarity between the two entities. There's no starting point of connection, and to the extent that it is a metaphor, it's an absurdist one.

But difference is necessary too. Consider: *The stove spewed clouds of black soot, a stove spewing clouds of black soot in our kitchen.* Here, the stove evokes nothing but itself, the sentence creating not so much a metaphor as a statement on actuality, a tautology. And perhaps, ultimately, this too is absurdist.

Septimus and Clarissa have a balance of similarity and difference that makes it possible for them to be in a metaphoric relationship. It is neither absurd nor reductive to allow the symbolic back-and-forth of their like and unlike qualities (and histories) to inform our understanding of both, and that is the best characterization I have for how these two work together in my mind as I read, and process, and contemplate, and remember the book.

To be clear, before I started writing a chapter on the subject, very little of this took place on a conscious level. Just as I do not say to myself, "I am looking at the stove differently now because of the mention of that dragon," I am not entirely conscious of the process through which these two characters mingle in my mind, shift my understanding of one another, and alter my impressions. I just know that they do. And again, just as I cannot quantify the dragonness of the stove after I hear that metaphor, I have no quantifications for the Septimusness of Clarissa, or visa versa, but I know that the process occurs.

To begin with love and its loss, little in this book makes me sadder than the fates of Clarissa's love for Sally Seton and of the officer named Evans who meant the world to Septimus. Each relationship starts with a genuine sweetness that Woolf rarely otherwise displays in this novel. She describes Septimus and Evans as, "two dogs playing on a hearth-rug; one worrying a paper screw, snarling, snapping, giving a pinch, now and then, at the old dog's ear; the other lying somnolent, blinking at the fire, raising a paw, turning and growling good-temperedly."

By the time I first read this description, I had already

encountered Clarissa's feelings for Sally, the kiss that Clarissa remembers as the "most exquisite moment of her life," the pleasure Clarissa took at just being in the same house with Sally: "'She is beneath this roof. . . . She is beneath this roof!'" I am certain that Clarissa's unambiguously romantic feelings for Sally (notwithstanding latter-day Clarissa's wavering about their nature) primed me to view the pairing of Evans and Septimus, which is less explicitly so, as also romantic, also erotic.

It is not as though Woolf writes: *He had Evans, a Sally Seton figure in his life.* The facts of same sex intimacy described in uniquely sweet and joyful terms, a truncated relationship, and a subsequent marriage to a member of the other sex soon after, are the similarities that form initial connectors for me so that in my mind these two relationships can begin to speak to one another.

Here is Clarissa, describing Peter Walsh's interruption of "the most exquisite moment of her whole life," the moment of Sally Seton's kiss: "'Star-gazing?' said Peter.

> It was like running one's face against a granite wall in the darkness! It was shocking; it was horrible!
>
> Not for herself. She felt only how Sally was

> being mauled already, maltreated; she felt his hostility; his jealousy; his determination to break into their companionship. All this she saw as one sees a landscape in a flash of lightning—and Sally (never had she admired her so much!) gallantly taking her way unvanquished.

Evans is literally killed, while Sally lives on, but the language in which Clarissa experiences the intrusion of one of her male suitors into her ecstasy at Sally's kiss, casts it as a shocking and physically painful moment for her—"running one's face against a granite wall in the darkness"(speaking of metaphors) and, further, as an act of violence against Sally, "mauled," "mistreated." That language and that imagery forms another connector between the two losses. The metaphorical violence in Clarissa's thoughts evokes the true violence of Evans's death, so that I begin to feel the presence of literal violence in my thoughts about the limitations of Clarissa's romance with Sally. And, in turn, the societal violence that prevents Clarissa from pursuing—or even clearly perceiving—the love and desire she feels for Sally, begins to seep over into my thoughts on Septimus and Evans so that even though I know that Evans is killed in battle, somewhere in my imagination there is a tinge of societal prohibition to the end of his and Septimus's relationship as well, not because I literally think that is what happened, but through the drift and weave of how metaphors function.

Another point of connection between Clarissa and Septimus is marital sex, not remembered sex, nor desired sex, but current sex—or, in both cases, the absence of it. Both are now celibate, both in some way aware of disappointing their partner.

And of course there are differences in this area, too. When it comes to sex with her husband, Clarissa has always been *just not that into it*, as we might now say: "Lovely in girlhood, suddenly there came a moment—for example on the river beneath the woods at Clieveden—when, through some contraction of this cold spirit, she had failed him. And then at Constantinople, and again and again."

And now, post childbearing years, post illness, she has taken the step of leaving the marital bed: "And really she preferred to read of the retreat from Moscow. [Richard] knew it. So the room was an attic; the bed narrow; and lying there reading, for she slept badly, she could not dispel a virginity preserved through childbirth which clung to her like a sheet."

Septimus, whose wife pleads with him to conceive a child with her, will not. His reasoning, which is not reasoning at all but reaction, is triangulated off the literature he once loved and now sees as carrying different truths:

> Love between man and woman was repulsive to Shakespeare. The business of copulation was filth to him before the end. But, Rezia said, she must have children. They had been married five years . . .

He thinks in terms of repulsion and filth, while Clarissa claims an inherently virginal nature undisturbed, unpenetrated, by the "getting of children." What he will not do, she feels in some sense that she has never done—though she has. What is vile to him is something closer to forgettable to her.

There is no confusion between their perspectives—but there is, again, a conversation between them, because these difference exist atop similarities. And so, because there is enough there for me to connect the two situations, Septimus's revolted reactions (unconvincingly attributed to Shakespeare) to "copulation" and "love between man and woman" can speak to Clarissa's "contraction of cold spirit."

Again, they are not to be confused, nor are they even different points on a trajectory. His feelings, his life experiences are not more dramatic versions of hers. They don't have to be in order to begin to seep into my thoughts about her. I know that a dragon isn't a stove, nor even a pumped up version of one, but because heat is a shared aspect of both, because so is the capacity to emit smoke, the dragon's qualities fall naturally into conversation with those of the stove, a conversation that I overhear and that changes my sense of the stove's possibilities. And so, I find myself wondering if Clarissa too isn't a bit repulsed by the sexual experiences she has had with her husband, and if Septimus hasn't always been a bit indifferent to it with his wife.

And of course, because each has had a romantic relationship with a member of their own sex, I also find myself wondering whether their respective steps away from marital relations are rooted in that experience and in those desires.

I find myself wondering.

That is the key phrase, for both reader and writer. If, as a reader, you don't find yourself wondering about aspects of a book, if, as a writer you don't create the room for that, the experience has a paucity to it, the collaboration likely a failure. But clearly there is no such failure here.

Though to be clear, the collaboration required—or maybe inspired—by *Mrs. Dalloway* is not an easy one. This novel, more than any other book I have read or, rather, finished (ahem, *Ulysses* . . .), leaves me always unsure I have found the right answer, read it correctly, reached the core of what Woolf means us to understand; and I'm not sure the opacity is unintentional. I often feel that Woolf has purposely designed a novel that defies interpretation while relying on interpretation as the primary engine of understanding it. And certainly there is something to be said for a work of fiction that requires endless engagement, even endless argument, rather than mere consumption. I have always said that my goal was to write for the second reading of my work, not the first, because I hoped there was a deeper layer that would be revealed that time through. I don't know that I ever succeeded with that goal, but I will say for Woolf, I have read this book, and read this book, and I discover new aspects every time. I have changed my mind about its meaning over and over. And the only way that happens is if the writer resists controlling every aspect. Woolf has done that here. She has resisted directing us to view things in a particular light, to an extraordinary degree. But more than that, she has constructed an entire symbolic system, at the core of the book, one that encourages us to involve our imaginations and our powers of interpretation constantly.

A danger of doing this, as I mentioned, lies in not achieving that balance between frustrating obscurity and excessive explanation. Woolf, for me, gets that right—in part because of the complexity of the systems she sets up. As I said, she is not going for simple contrasts here. One can imagine a book in which "doubles" are so obviously opposites that all a reader need do is draw easy conclusions about what the author is trying to do. This is not that book. Even once we know that Septimus is "intended" to be Clarissa's double, we must work hard to understand the implications of that relationship; and very little of what we each, individually, glean, can be absolute.

For me, what saves Woolf here from the charge of excessive obscurity, in spite of the perpetual sense I have of theorizing, rather than reaching conclusions, is that the doubling itself is, in fact, very clear. As an interpretive reader of this novel, I always feel that I have a solid platform from which to investigate the more nuanced and, frankly, murky parts of the book, just as I always sense that doing so yields more, if not complete, understanding. Again, Woolf does not give us the task of trying to understand a stove better by comparing it to frog. There is always enough connection here for me to feel that the work of trying to unearth Woolf's mission with this novel, and with this particular literary device, pays off. Not with complete understanding, ever, but with increasingly compelling possibilities.

To be clear, this all goes beyond these exchanges of characteristics I have described as metaphoric. The novel is full of references from one storyline to the other, overlaps of symbolism, seemingly mystical connections and coincidences. Just before Septimus dies, his thoughts take this form:

> Now for his writings; how the dead sing behind rhododendron bushes; odes to Time; conversations with Shakespeare; Evans, Evans, Evans—his messages from the dead; do not cut down trees; tell the Prime Minister. Universal love: the meaning of the world. Burn them! he cried.

Is one of the messages from the dead, "do not cut down

trees?" Or is that a separate thought he had? If the former, is that message from Clarissa's sister Sylvia on whom a tree fell? Is Septimus's emphasis on trees from early in the book, meant to draw our thoughts to that poor long-dead girl, and therefore help us connect Septimus's "insane" ramblings to Clarissa?

Earlier in the same scene, Lucrezia and Septimus play around the wrongness of a hat she is making and find a moment of normalcy in the exchange, imagining the woman whose hat is wrong. The novel begins with Clarissa worrying that there is something wrong about her hat. What is the connection? What is Woolf asking us to see? Or is there no point? Is it just a coincidence?

I haven't given anything like an exhaustive list here of my experiences with these two characters as they interact in my mind and alter my perceptions of one another, and offer up clues that may sometimes be red herrings—or not—inviting me to theorize about these doubles, and so ultimately theorize about what Woolf herself is trying to say. Was Clarissa in some way numbed by her sister's death, as Septimus was by the death of Evans? Is Septimus's guilt over this "crime" a reason to look for a corresponding guilt in Clarissa? A corresponding crime? I wonder, I wonder, I wonder. And then there is more about which I wonder, and there will be more after that. And then more. And, for all my uncertainty about much in this book, I am pretty sure that all that wondering is another thing Woolf intended. In fact, our wondering may well be the point.

3. Social Commentary

Less of an area for wondering, Woolf clearly and effectively uses the character of Septimus Warren Smith as a vehicle for her anti-war sentiment, and also for the condemnation of the inhumane mental health care available. What has been less obvious to me and has puzzled me, is what exactly that has to do with his being Clarissa's "double." It felt very unlike Woolf for this not all to connect in some way beyond the most obvious contrasts: he went to war, she didn't; he needed a good psychologist in order to survive the day, she didn't. So I set about looking for the same sort of connectors that have so influenced my understanding in other areas, to see if Woolf had, again, set up a scheme for her readers to follow, and I found that she had.

And this time, unsurprisingly, it is all about death.

Septimus has returned from the horrors of daily slaughter,

the fears, the losses, the brutality, transformed. I have come to think of him as something like that dragon in the kitchen. So altered is he by the inhuman landscape of the war, that he might as well be from another reality, one with different rules about what is acceptable, what it is necessary to do to survive, with a different value placed on human life, and a different scale of violence and of loss. His experiences have made it so that he is no longer suited to the gentility of the world in which we find him, Clarissa Dalloway's London, any more than an actual dragon belongs in the kitchen of my New York apartment. There is no place for him in "normal" society, because he no longer functions within the reality of those who set the rules.

Distinct from all else that is going on with these two characters, Woolf wanted us to see clearly and with our emotions fully aroused that the nation that demanded of young people that they fight, did not then accommodate the drastic changes that demand wrought in them, the damage it did to them. To skip over the deeply felt anti-war sentiment in this book is to do it, and Woolf, and probably ourselves a disservice. And as shocking as it is to read about this kind of neglect and this failure to care for veterans in 1923, it is even worse that these problems continue, as they do. (And, most recently, the practice of viewing those on the frontlines as disposable can be seen in the context of the health care workers whose trauma in this pandemic is inadequately noticed, poorly understood, and taken for granted.)

Clarissa has also known death in her life. Her parents are gone, and more relevantly, I think, there is the accidental death of her sister Sylvia, from a tree falling on her. That death provides me with one of those connectors between Clarissa and Septimus, a jumping off point for understanding more fully the impact of having these characters as "doubles."

We never learn of Sylvia's death from Clarissa, we only get this, through Peter's memories and thoughts:

> . . . possibly [Clarissa] said to herself, As we are a doomed race, chained to a sinking ship . . . as the whole thing is a bad joke, let us, at any rate, do our part; mitigate the sufferings of our fellow-prisoners . . . decorate the dungeon with flowers and air-cushions; be as decent as we possibly can. Those ruffians, the Gods, shan't have it all their own way,—her notion being that the Gods, who never lost a chance of hurting, thwarting and spoiling human lives were seriously put out if, all the same,

> you behaved like a lady. That phase came directly after Sylvia's death—that horrible affair. To see your own sister killed by a falling tree (all Justin Parry's fault—all his carelessness) before your very eyes, a girl too on the verge of life, the most gifted of them, Clarissa always said, was enough to turn one bitter. Later she wasn't so positive perhaps; she thought there were no Gods; no one was to blame; and so she evolved this atheist's religion of doing good for the sake of goodness."

The real connector between Clarissa and Septimus is not death exactly, but the concern over life's meaning in its shadow. Clarissa, who does not believe in any of the traditional religions, has devised a way to give life whatever meaning she can: Flowers, décor, ladylike behavior, and doing good toward others, "mitigating the sufferings of our fellow-prisoners." Those were her thoughts as a very young woman, and indeed this is the life we find her leading. Flowers: check. Décor: check. Ladylike behavior: check. And as for mitigating the suffering of others, I believe that this is what those parties of hers are all about.

> An offering for the sake of offering, perhaps. Anyhow, it was her gift. Nothing else had she of the slightest importance; could not think, write, even play the piano. She muddled Armenians and Turks; loved success; hated discomfort; must be liked; talked oceans of nonsense: and to this day, ask her what the Equator was, and she did not know. All the same, that one day should follow another; Wednesday, Thursday, Friday, Saturday; that one should wake up in the morning; see the sky; walk in the park; meet Hugh Whitbread; then suddenly in came Peter; then these roses; it was enough. After that, how unbelievable death was!—that it must end; and no one in the whole world would know how she had loved it all; how, every instant . . .

"An offering for the sake of offering," she calls them—echoing the phrase, "doing good for the sake of goodness." And, lest we miss the religious implications, she uses the word "offering" four times in the course of three paragraphs.

"After that how unbelievable death was," Clarissa thinks. There are two ways to read this line. One is, "Oh, how unbelievable that we all must die!" The other is that through these activities, she has given herself some relief from believing in death, has rendered it literally, if only momentarily, "unbelievable."

Clarissa's belief system, the parties, the flowers, all of it, existing, as belief systems tend to, in response to the fact of mortality, has everything to do with the society in which she lives. Her "offerings" of parties are not only social, which they are, but are inherently tied in with the height of the very society into which Septimus can no longer fit.

Septimus, exposed to all the attendant grotesquery of war, can find neither solace in nor help from that society "It might be possible, Septimus thought, looking at England from the train window, as they left Newhaven; it might be possible that the world itself is without meaning." He is beyond the comforts of flowers, and parties, of décor.

There is a poignant and relevant moment when, having resolved to die, Septimus, runs through his possible means:

> Getting up rather unsteadily, hopping indeed from foot to foot, he considered Mrs. Filmer's nice clean bread knife with "Bread" carved on the handle. Ah, but one mustn't spoil that. The gas fire? But it was too late now. Holmes was coming. Razors he

> might have got, but Rezia, who always did that sort of thing, had packed them. There remained only the window, the large Bloomsbury-lodging house window, the tiresome, the troublesome, and rather melodramatic business of opening the window and throwing himself out.

For this moment, it almost seems that worries about etiquette and what "one does," might save him. One must not ruin the bread knife, he thinks; he recognizes the possibility of "melodrama," imagines, in socially conscious terms, being viewed. And he doesn't sound the least bit mad here. He sounds oddly mundane. But though this vestige of thinking about social norms feels like a possible turning point, the charge of Holmes up the stairs is enough to reinforce his knowledge that there is no place for him in this society.

In response to news of the war veteran's death, Clarissa has a turning point of her own, in the other direction:

> She felt somehow very like him—the young man who had killed himself. She felt glad that he had done it; thrown it away. The clock was striking. The

> leaden circles dissolved in the air. He made her feel the beauty; made her feel the fun. But she must go back. She must assemble. She must find Sally and Peter. And she came in from the little room.

Since I began to see the dynamics I describe above, Clarissa's reliance on society's pleasures and niceties and kindnesses as a religion of sorts, a way of combating the awfulness of mortality, and society's reliance on destroying certain of its citizens in order to allow those niceties to continue, I have been unable to read this passage as anything other than Clarissa repeating that pattern. The final destruction of Septimus at his own hand, which is an extension of the war and also of society's failure to care for those who sacrificed for its continuation, seemingly makes Clarissa feel again how beautiful and fun her own life can be—and so she rejoins society, in the form of the party, reasserting her belief in her "offering," reaffirming its power to comfort her.

Though, to be clear, I read that line about "beauty and fun" in a very specific way. I think his death scares her, reminds of her own mortality, and it isn't that she *feels* the beauty and fun as the most obvious sense, as much as that, as a result of having to contemplate death, she *remembers* them. And fun and beauty are not small things for her; they are her religion. Flowers, décor, and parties—beauty and fun—are the way she manages to make something meaningful of this life.

As for her feeling "somehow very like him, the young man who had killed himself," one possibility is that she feels like him because she is like him. She thinks of whether life is worth living, struggles with that. They are also alike in sharing the same societal system, albeit from very different postions, their lives determined by the same rules and inhumanities. She is no less a part of an England that relies on the horrors of war to perpetuate itself than he is, and in that way, if one takes this to its extreme, she is also "very like" Septimus because, as a member of that society, she too has had a hand in killing him.

Does that mean that Woolf ultimately uses Septimus to condemn Clarissa? The most problematic line here is the one about her being "glad" he did it. Is she glad he did it because in fact his killing himself made her think life is fun? If so, then yes, Woolf has used Septimus to condemn Clarissa. She could be glad he did it as an assertion of free will. But I suspect that what is meant here is that she is glad he did it, because she understands that he could not find the comforts she has been able to find. That is my best (and most generous) guess. It is today's guess. I admit though that there have been other times through when I have just detested her at this point. The phrase "solipsistic jerk" may have been scribbled in my margin, along the way.

But not today. Today, I think that the point is to condemn society, and to present both Clarissa and Septimus, from start to finish, as trapped in that system. He certainly gets the worst of it, they do not suffer equally, but they are equally trapped.

And perhaps she is simply glad for him that he got out.

I'm sure I have missed a lot of what this doubling of Woolf's does for this book. Still, speaking as both a reader and a writer, if this is "all" she got out of that single device, it would be enough. (*Dayenu*, as we say at Passover, every year.) And that makes me glad, because there is a bit of a secret reason why I wanted to prove—to myself—that the addition of Septimus was not just an impulsive or pasted-on way of making the book seem larger, nor a device for the sake of having a device, but a necessary and critical piece of the book's central meaning, and of the experience of reading it.

You see, ever since I first learned that he wasn't there all along, I have had a fear. I have feared that Woolf herself feared—or knew—that a book about a woman giving a party, no matter how much that woman might think about death, or even commit suicide at the end (or merely die), would not be viewed as being as important or as much of an intellectual product as a book with a man in it.

I have certainly had that thought myself, about my own work

And I have further feared that she also believed—or maybe knew—that it would be hard to make the "insanity" of an affluent woman of enormous privilege sympathetic; that people would wonder what right Clarissa Dalloway had to be mad. So she invented a man who had "earned" his madness in an easily understandable way, an entirely sympathetic way. And of course, I feared this, because it saddens me to think that Woolf may well have thought that about herself—that she had no "right" to suffer from mental illness when she had so much privilege in her life.

I have certainly had that thought about myself.

But then, worries, anxieties, knowledge about the biases of the world, all of that is there for us all as we sit down to write. The best we can hope for is that the work will somehow, magically be held aloft by exactly those thing and more, by the author's own unique collection neuroses and gifts, by their self-consciousness and their generosity.

Maybe some concerns about sexism and limited compassion did lurk behind Woolf's creation of Septimus Warren Smith. Perhaps she put in that disclosure about his being "intended" to be Clarissa's double, because that is not in fact how he came to be. Maybe she was covering for motives that felt less than purely literary. It is unknowable, at this point. And I'm not sure that it matters anyway. Septimus is a key to this book, no less than is Clarissa herself. They are a pair of keys, a pair of mismatched keys that somehow still work the same lock. Just as Woolf intended them to be.

Three

OF STREAMS, OF OCEANS, OF CONSCIOUSNESS

"I adumbrate here a study of insanity and suicide; the world seen by the sane and the insane side by side."

—Virginia Woolf, Diary Entry, October 14, 1922

FIRST, A STORY.

In 1981, when I was eighteen, I boarded a train going from Grand Central Station in New York to New Haven, to home. Those Conrail trains were shabby, ramshackle monsters, swaying, shuddering, lights blinking on and off. Maybe they still are; I haven't been on one in years. I believe we even smoked on them back then, a fact that places the whole experience in some incomprehensible, reckless past. The night in question fell in February, cold, bitter, one of those record setting lows kind of nights. I boarded the train from the platform, and had settled onto my torn vinyl seat, the heat scant but making things bearable, when a door slid open and stayed that way, stuck, frigid air pouring immediately, painfully inside.

Within maybe a minute, the conductor had pried the door shut again and fastened it. And soon we rolled away. And as we did, I thought about the fact that while that cold air had blasted us all, for at least few seconds there, every person in the car was thinking the same thing—or some version of it: *Cold. I'm cold.*

Our thoughts, the thoughts of a couple of dozen strangers, had merged for those moments, pulling us out of the peculiarity of our own individual musings, out of our particular identities into something like a collective consciousness.

Some of us may have dressed more warmly than others, some might simply mind cold air less, but for a moment there, we all had essentially the same extreme experience and, because of that extremity, the same thought: *Cold!*

And then of course we settled back into whatever we had been doing before, a kind of barely noticeable return to all the things that distinguish one person from another, a hasty retreat into the peculiar specificities, idiosyncrasies, concerns, and delights of one's own stream of consciousness—a term coined by William James, some time before the literary set grabbed onto it.

If you have ever been in a widespread power outage, you have doubtless experienced something similar. An entire city thinks at once: *The lights have gone out*. Bad turbulence on a plane has the same effect, the intrusion of a single thought into a hundred heads. The sound of a bomb exploding. Instants of disruption, disruption of the notion that we are safe, disruption to physical comfort. Moments of sensory assault. Because for all our differences and individuality there are phenomena that demolish some of that, if only momentarily—much as I experienced that long-ago night with a blast of cold air on a Conrail train.

Memories of that night have popped into my thoughts from time to time through the years. It was an experience that etched itself into me, joining the rotation of scenes and moments that flit across my consciousness now and then. But as I've been immersed in *Mrs. Dalloway* this past year, the memory has become more frequent, that sensation of oneness with others, the connection within a crowd, tugging at me, as if for attention.

Back in those days, my college years, I mostly went home to New Haven for therapy, seeing the psychiatrist I had started to see when sixteen. What sent me to her originally was a relentless unhappiness, a sense of desperation. I was failing at school, struggling socially, and just miserable. I don't remember very much about what we covered in those earliest months, but I remember something we didn't cover. After I'd been seeing her for about a year, she brought my father up. "You have barely mentioned him," she said. "I know you have one, he's pretty well known. I see him around town. But if I go by what you've said to me, he isn't really a part of your life."

This was the father who was institutionalized when I was eight, the father around whose emotional fragilities and highs and lows our entire household revolved. The father I very much feared being like and also longed to be like, as I picked and chose among his stellar and his terrifying characteristics. Yes, please, let me be brilliant and charismatic and successful. But if it's all the same, I'll pass on the hellacious temper, the stint in a mental ward, the depression, the alcoholism.

"I really don't think he's a problem," I told my doctor at the time.

There are so many jokes about it being what we avoid

that carries the most weight, about how therapists frame our dodges and avoidance that way. It's a cliché, the stuff of sitcom humor. So it's unnerving, embarrassing, to look back at seventeen-year-old me and see the degree to which I enacted that cliché, the degree to which I felt it.

He has nothing to do with my unhappiness.

At that time, my conscious feelings about my father, the story I told myself, were that he was—always this came first—a Genius, a status that to my mind carried unlimited rights and no responsibilities, a status that bought him the freedom not to parent me in anything like an acceptable way, and therefore, through some twisty transitive process, meant that his rages, the demands of his emotional illness and addiction, would have, did have, no impact on me.

He was something like an extra person in our family, a presence that drew a massive amount of attention from my mother, necessary to keep him from raging at her and at us. He could be extravagantly affectionate—or maybe rhetorically affectionate is the better phrase. Rhetorically, extravagantly affectionate. He loved us, loved me, but his temper and the demands of his mental illness meant that his love could not be experienced as anything like unconditional. I was loved as long as I followed the rules, the central one being that he came first.

As a child I felt myself to be a minor figure in his narrative, my primary identity being his daughter; my primary focus, him. He defined my young life, even while not being a part of the daily life I lived in school, with friends, with TV shows, the normal bits. He was a phenomenon of dramatic highs and lows more than he was a father to me.

And to my mind he had nothing to do with the deep sadness and anger that drove me into therapy at the age of sixteen. Or with why, two years later, I was boarding trains in New York, interrupting my college life twice weekly to return to that therapist, or with why I was so keenly and wistfully aware of being part of a small group of people all sharing the same thought, even if it was just for a moment, even if it was just the single word, *cold*.

When I first heard the term "stream of consciousness"—in high school, so a bit before that train ride—I somehow got the sense[3] that it referred to just that sort of merging of consciousnesses, that meeting of minds; as though there were

3. A shocking amount of my learning as a young person can be described as "somehow getting the sense . . ." I suspect this is true of many who have AD(H)D.

a universal stream of thought into which we all occasionally dip, and in which we encounter one another from time to time. The stream of shared consciousness.

Of course this is not at all what the term means, neither as psychologist William James first conceived it nor as those who apply the term to literature have used it for the past century and more. In fact, I didn't just have the meaning wrong, I had it exactly wrong, perfectly wrong. The term *stream of consciousness* refers to something internal, personal, individual, our own thoughts, all the time, every one of them, that which, in fact, distinguishes me from you in some very vital way. Nothing to do with sharing or merging or meeting of any kind.

In literature the term stream of consciousness refers to a character's inner monologue—and then also, as a technique, to a narrator's capacity to dip in and out of that flow, thus creating a third person narrative that feels more natural, more like how people experience existence than other more formal, distant narrative modes.

Virginia Woolf was what we now call an early adaptor of this method of narration, and *Mrs. Dalloway* is often cited as a primary, important example. Essentially every paragraph of the novel stands as an example of this technique. Here is

Peter Walsh:

> He pulled off his boots. He emptied his pockets. Out came with his pocket-knife a snapshot of Daisy on the verandah; Daisy all in white, with a fox-terrier on her knee; very charming, very dark; the best he had ever seen of her. It did come, after all so naturally; so much more naturally than Clarissa. No fuss. No bother. No finicking and fidgeting. All plain sailing.

To the extent that Woolf has a traditional narrator, it mostly[4] exists to give what amount to stage directions: "He pulled off his boots. He emptied his pockets." The emotional content, as well as what I think of as the music of the prose all come from Peter's thoughts. "It did come, after all so

4. The most significant example of Woolf employing a traditional narrator comes when she gives us Septimus's life story. A sentence like "London has swallowed up many millions of young men called Smith; thought nothing of fantastic Christian names like Septimus with which their parents have thought to distinguish them" is obviously not something Septimus is thinking. The most likely reason for this choice is that, in Septimus, Woolf has created a character whose own thoughts and memories are not coherent enough to give us a clear history. It is one of the many ways she distinguishes his mental state, and I find it a fascinating traditional narrative island in the novel.

naturally; so much more naturally than Clarissa. No fuss. No bother. No finicking and fidgeting. All plain sailing."

Here, we are in Richard Dalloway's thoughts, complete with a dialogue he is having with himself. Woolf often employs this technique of questions—*Flowers?*—to place us in the character's thoughts and keep us there with a process of unfolding realization that is not at all the province of traditional distant narrators:

> But he wanted to come in holding something. Flowers? Yes, flowers, since he did not trust his taste in gold; any number of flowers, roses, orchids, to celebrate what was, reckoning things as you will, an event; this feeling about her when they spoke of Peter Walsh at luncheon . . .

Woolf not only uses stream of consciousness for the purposes described above, but also to provide extensive "back story" and, in essence, make sequential first person narrators of her characters. In her journal, she wrote: "It took me a year's groping to discover what I call my tunneling process, by which I tell the past by installments, as I have need of it. This is my prime discovery so far." (15, Oct 1923)

That word "tunneling" is so evocative, implying as it does that Woolf is moving *toward* those figures, indeed tunneling through them, allowing the stories to emanate from them, from their stored recollections, rather than using a more traditional distant omniscient narrator who has the capacity to tell us facts from a distance. One can feel an almost physical shift in this change. The weight of a character's personal history is no longer the property of a narrator who holds it in some neutral space, but is carried by the character, exists within them, and it is the author's role to unearth it, the narrator's role only to provide a kind of neutral space in which these tunnels are exposed, as needed. Here is Peter Walsh again:

> . . . [H]e saw her most often at Bourton, in the late summer, when he stayed there for a week, or fortnight even, as people did in those days. First on top of some hill there she would stand, hands clapped to her hair, her cloak blowing out, pointing, crying to them—she saw the Severn beneath. Or in a wood, making the kettle boil—very ineffective with her fingers . . .

As these musings continue, we stay well and firmly within the tunnel constructed of Peter's life, or perhaps more accurately of his memories of that life, a tunnel that is his alone, to which narrator and reader alike are guests.

By the time I read *Mrs. Dalloway* in graduate school, I understood—decently enough—what stream of consciousness was, and knew that Woolf employed it in this novel, but had no clue that she also explores aspects of overlapping consciousnesses, oceans of shared consciousness; nor what that might have to with her depiction of "the world seen by the sane and insane side by side;" nor what it might have to do with me.

The assignment for my *Mrs. Dalloway* class included writing a short paper on a craft aspect of the book. These papers, called annotations, typically involved analyzing how an author accomplishes something that you have found difficult in your own work. I wrote many annotations on such things as how authors end short stories, and on dialogue, and on my old challenge, descriptive passages. For *Mrs. Dalloway*, I wrote about how Woolf switches point of view from one character to another.

It's a tricky business with which all writers who take

on omniscient narration must contend. If you are "in the head" of one character and too abruptly change that focus to another character it can be jarring to a reader, reminding them that there's an author who is orchestrating all of this.

Woolf's solution, not invariable but frequent, is to do what I think of as triangulating the two (or more) consciousnesses off of an object or other entity, sometimes off of a thought. Here, Peter Walsh and Clarissa are in her drawing room together:

> And this has been going on all the time! he thought; week after week; Clarissa's life; while I—he thought; and at once everything seemed to radiate from him; journeys; rides; quarrels; adventures; bridge parties; love affairs; work; work, work! and he took out his knife quite openly—his old horn-handled knife which Clarissa could swear he had had these thirty years—and clenched his fist upon it.
>
> What an extraordinary habit that was, Clarissa thought; always playing with a knife. Always making one feel, too, frivolous; empty-minded; a mere silly chatterbox, as he used . . .

We are in Peter's thoughts as he withdraws his knife, and then in Clarissa's as she reacts to the knife. The knife is a point of connection between them, or of triangulation, as I think of it.

My first reaction to detecting this technique was a kind of head-shaking amazement at how simple it was. What an elegant solution for something so boggling to so many of us! In my annotation, I described this point of view shifting as passing a "baton of consciousness," thinking this was very original of me, only to run across the phrase in relation *Mrs. Dalloway* multiple times in the ensuing years—because that is so clearly what she is doing. Most importantly, I thought of it as only a craft technique, with no greater implications beyond deftly handling a challenge inherent to omniscient narration.

Over time though, as I read and reread, *Mrs. Dalloway,* an odd thing happened, and I began to see that transfer, that point of triangulation, not simply as a writer's technique, and no longer as a passing of a baton, but as an actual merger of two (or more) consciousnesses. I started picturing the thoughts of the characters as physical presences in the scene, as if Clarissa's and Peter's thoughts were thought-bubbles, those bubbles overlapping for just that moment, the shared awareness of the pocket knife not a trick, but a phenomenon. The consciousnesses which I had assumed to be entirely distinct began to blur at their boundaries.

In this passage, which employs a variant of that triangulation, there's more than a hint of that porousness to thought:

> [Elizabeth]stood quite still and looked at her mother; but the door was ajar, and outside the door was Miss Kilman, as Clarissa knew; Miss Kilman in her mackintosh, listening to whatever they said.
>
> Yes, Miss Kilman stood on the landing, and wore a mackintosh; but had her reasons. First, it was cheap; second, she was over forty; and did not, after all, dress to please. She was poor, moreover; degradingly poor. Otherwise she would not be taking jobs from people like the Dalloways; from rich people, who liked to be kind. Mr. Dalloway, to do him justice, had been kind. But Mrs. Dalloway had not. She had been merely condescending. She came from the most worthless of all classes—the rich, with a smattering of culture. They had expensive things everywhere; pictures, carpets, lots

> of servants. She considered that she had a perfect right to anything that the Dalloways did for her.

The mackintosh is the point of connection, and though the sentence beginning "Yes, Miss Kilman stood on the landing, and wore a mackintosh. . ." seems to be from the point of view of the narrator, with that litany of her "reasons," the paragraph slides seamlessly from that into Miss Kilman's thoughts: "Mr. Dalloway, to do him justice, had been kind . . ." The overall effect is of Elizabeth's awareness of Miss Kilman's presence transferring to Clarissa ("as Clarissa knew") and Clarissa's disdain for Miss Kilman's mackintosh prompting Miss Kilman's thoughts on that very subject, as we are told first that she "had her reasons" and then those reasons are expressed through her thoughts on them.

This blurring occurs on a larger scale as well, as here in reaction the backfire of a car, thought to be carrying a "royal personage" or some such dignitary:

> . . . rumours were at once in circulation from the middle of Bond Street to Oxford Street on one side, to Atkinson's scent shop on the other, passing

> invisibly, inaudibly, like a cloud, swift, veil-like upon hills, falling indeed with something of a cloud's sudden sobriety and stillness upon faces which a second before had been utterly disorderly . . . But now mystery had brushed them with her wing; they had heard the voice of authority; the spirit of religion was abroad with her eyes bandaged tight and her lips gaping wide.

In this moment, we take a leap from the depths and individuality of Clarissa Dalloway's impressions and memories, into something very much more like a shared consciousness. The bang of the car rivets mass attention, and the spectacle of some person of presumed importance creates a curiosity that has the effect of demolishing individuality. Those "faces which a second before had been utterly disorderly" immediately share the same curiosity, the same response to "the voice of authority," the same ignorance; and ultimately, the same awareness of what authority, society, and obligation have wrought:

> For thirty seconds all heads were inclined the same way—to the window. Choosing a pair of

> gloves—should they be to the elbow or above it, lemon or pale grey?—ladies stopped; when the sentence was finished something had happened. Something so trifling in single instances that no mathematical instrument, though capable of transmitting shocks in China, could register the vibration; yet in its fulness rather formidable and in its common appeal emotional; for in all the hat shops and tailors' shops strangers looked at each other and thought of the dead; of the flag; of Empire . . . In a public house in a back street a Colonial insulted the House of Windsor which led to words, broken beer glasses, and a general shindy, which echoed strangely across the way in the ears of girls buying white underlinen threaded with pure white ribbon for their weddings. For the surface agitation of the passing car as it sunk grazed something very profound.

My own experience of a momentary shared thought in a crowd—"*cold!*"—was relatively insignificant. But here we have something, to borrow Woolf's words, very profound. This is a society five years out from a devastating war, from a shared sense of horror and of bereavement, and from the subsuming of individual needs to those of the nation. And though, perhaps, with passing time, the war is no longer the first thing on everyone's mind, it has left a shared vulnerability that has the power to erase individuality, as if in a reprise of the wartime state of mind. One moment you are a woman weighing your own very particular taste in gloves, and the next you are part of a single consciousness, remembering.

Though there is an exception. We first meet Septimus Warren Smith between the two passages quoted above, his attention riveted by the car, but in a very different way:

> And there the motor car stood, with drawn blinds . . . The world wavered and quivered and threatened to burst into flames. It is I who am blocking the way, he thought. Was he not being looked at and pointed at; was he not weighted there, rooted to the pavement, for a purpose? But for what purpose?

It is I who am blocking the way, he thought. While the crowd speculates with one mind about the identity of the car's occupant, Septimus instead confuses the object of their attention, the clear center of attention, with himself. This is the first enacted sign of his emotional instability that we have, our first sure clue that he doesn't perceive the world as others do. Confused about whether he is the viewer or the viewed, the inconvenienced or the impediment, he does not, cannot, participate in the shared consciousness of the moment. He is out of step on this most defining level.

We see him do something similar, some pages later, when an airplane appears, writing letters in the sky, and the crowd wonders what the letters might be. Septimus, who we have now learned has threatened suicide, cannot adopt the shared perspective. His wife points the plane out to him:

> 'Look, look, Septimus!' she cried. For Dr. Holmes had told her to make her husband (who had nothing whatever seriously the matter with him but was a little out of sorts) take an interest in things outside himself.
>
> So, thought Septimus, looking up, they are signalling to me . . . signalling their intention to provide him, for nothing, for ever, for looking merely, with beauty, more beauty! Tears ran down his cheeks.

Again, he sees himself where he is not, places himself at the center of this spectacle. Lucrezia, his wife, does not grasp that wherever he looks, he cannot "take an interest in things outside himself." It is as if, had he been on that New York train with me, his thought would not have been "Cold! I'm cold" but perhaps "I have caused this cold," or even "The cold has come to harm me alone."

And of course, Woolf has created a perfect, dramatized critique of the profession charged with helping such people as Septimus. Holmes has failed to grasp the most central aspect of how Septimus's very real ailment manifests.

"I adumbrate here a study of insanity and suicide; the world seen by the sane and the insane side by side," Woolf wrote. "[T]he world *seen by . . .*" is the key phrase here. Having been inside a head gripped by such an illness, having seen with eyes that cannot perceive what others do, she knows of what she speaks.

You don't expect a study of point of view in a novel to bring you back to a painful period of your own life. Point of View seems like such a dry subject, craft at its most irritatingly technical, evoking thoughts of angels and heads of pins. But Woolf breaks through the dryness, shatters the usual boundaries of such techniques, and uses what I think of as *extreme craft* to evoke something deeply human—and deeply personal to me.

•

I don't talk much about my years as an agoraphobe, the two decades when it was often hard for me to leave my house. I allude to that period in my book *Crash Course: Essays From Where Writing and Life Collide*, but don't go into the experience in any great detail. Even now, I have left the second sentence of this paragraph incomplete. It should read, ". . . the nearly two decades of my life when it was hard for me to leave my house because I was afraid there were people, specific people I encountered, who meant to do me harm."

The kind of terror I experienced on a near daily basis when I was unable just to hide in my home, was a full-body terror, a physical phenomenon, nothing intellectual about it, and there was nothing anyone could say to talk me down. I was beyond logic. If someone turned up in the pharmacy after I saw them an hour earlier in the grocery store, I assumed they were following me, and I was likely to abandon whatever I had collected in my cart, dart from the store, and take a circuitous route home. If a car made two turns behind me, following the same route, my heart would start pounding, and I would begin making unnecessary turns, or might even pull into a police station or a post office—though what I thought a postal worker could do to help is now beyond me.

There was no real content to what I feared from these poor uninterested strangers. I didn't fear physical harm. I just feared. It was akin to the sensations of a child who imagines there is a monster under their bed. (And in fact it was very like my own sensations as a child when I imagined there was a monster under my bed, which I frequently did.) Sheer panic with no narrative to match the terror, but with the accompanying sense that the danger grows out of a wrongness about oneself. There was something wrong about me, something bad, and that made the world a dangerous place.

The hallmark of these episodes is that I took innocent activities that had nothing to do with me and flipped them around so they were entirely about me. There was a warp to my view of the world. Every event, every setting, had the potential to be about a danger to me. A strange piece of garbage stuck in our driveway cans could set me off, throwing me into a panic, the content of which I couldn't articulate; while the more normal reaction, my husband's reaction, was,

"I really wish people wouldn't use our garbage cans."

The symptoms abated around activities that related to caring for my children, and peaked when I tried to create an identity beyond my domestic role. Writing in particular set me off, as I found myself unable to attend workshops I had joined, or finish any projects I began. The terror of possibly having my words out in the world shut me down.

At the time, I felt keenly that I was sabotaging myself, and just as keenly that I had no idea how to stop.

When the symptoms were bad, over periods of days or weeks, I wondered for how long I could bear it. I took some comfort in knowing that I could always "self-medicate" by simply—not so simply—remaining in my home, limiting all interactions with the world. This never fully stopped the symptoms, but did give me some relief; though that relief came at a high price: never accomplishing anything outside the confines of my home, never doing much that involved the outside world. But I wanted to be entirely invisible. I needed to erase myself. Only an existence of self-abnegation felt safe. For a very long time, my life was a choice between the terror of being in the world and the surrender of a cloistered and frustrated life in my own home. For a very long time, I chose the latter, and with that submission to my own emotional care, came a deep, searing grief.

I'll skip ahead a bit here, not detail more months and years of the same, to the spring of 2001, when I was thirty-nine. Two things happened in my life that May: My father died, and three weeks later I started writing again. And writing. And writing. That September, I joined a writing group and actually attended it. That first evening, when I got home, I bragged to my husband about having been "pretty much okay." We treated my sitting in a room with a dozen perfectly amiable strangers as if I had climbed a particularly intimidating mountain.

"I did it!" I said.

"I'm really proud of you," he said.

Sometimes, the first understanding you get of how ill you have been, comes as you are recovering.

It took me several years to detect the connection between the beginning of the end of my agoraphobia and my father's death; between my ability to write, to express myself in the world, and my father's death. During those years, I may well have needed not to see my new strength as the result of his absence. Loyalty is a tricky business, and for all the challenges my father brought into my life, I still have many loyalties toward him. Guilt is also a funny business, and had I let myself see that I could only "find my voice" once his was silenced, I might well have silenced myself again.

But time passes. It has been twenty years, and I long ago recognized the degree to which, unknown to him, unintended, his was an inhibiting presence in my life. I understand, too, the degree to which I created monsters first under the bed, and then in the car behind me, in the grocery store, largely out of long buried anger toward him, those adversaries forged of the very emotions I denied having to my psychiatrist all those many years ago.

Knowledge is power, I suppose, but it is often also something else. This late understanding of mine fills me with sadness, for myself, yes, but mostly for him. I know enough of what it is like to be at the mercy of mental illness to understand how little he meant to do the harm he did.

What followed that first evening at a writing group was two years of tremendous difficulty and also startling joy. I continued to attend that workshop. I went to readings. I went to a writing conference. I completed stories and submitted them for publication. I did these things accompanied by regular panic and terrors of the sort I had always known—but gradually, these episodes faded. Days of fear became the exception rather than the rule. I found some previously inaccessible strength, and an accompanying hope. I didn't know the term at the time, but by staying active in the world in spite of my fears, I had essentially put myself on a course of exposure therapy, and it was working.

In 2003, at the age of 41, I applied to graduate school and I got in—though on my first day, I almost quit. I arrived, parked my car, got out, walked toward the registration building, turned around, got back in my car and drove away. Here I was, on the brink of doing exactly what I had wanted to do for decades, literally decades, and I wasn't at all sure I could. The worst of my symptoms had mostly receded by then, but on that day, as though aware of their impending defeat, they reasserted themselves, so that I was again terrified of everything. I couldn't imagine what I was doing hundreds of miles from home. I couldn't believe I had thought I could be a student again, among strangers.

I drove my car a few miles from campus and went into a local museum. I stayed there until I convinced myself that if I gave in to this fear, it was all over. No graduate school, sure, but I was also certain that a step backwards of this magnitude would result in a full retreat, all gains lost. The weight of what felt like a defining self-betrayal would bury me.

After about an hour, I drove back to the school, parked the car, registered, and stayed.

Throughout my two years in the program, I never confided any of this to anyone. I may have joked about having been panicked about grad school, and may even have mentioned keeping myself sheltered for many years, but I never spoke about the paranoia, or the despair it brought on. It wasn't shame that kept me quiet, it was more a sense that my victory over my own symptoms was fragile and I didn't know what the impact of discussing them might be.

And of course they weren't entirely gone. I still had bad days, but those were increasingly crowded out by good ones—though the work of being okay enough to push through took a toll. I was an emotional wreck throughout my graduate school years. I was thin skinned, and easily hurt. I had mood swings that were dizzying. I felt the loss of all the years I'd spent hiding as an enormous pressure. I had an impossible game of catch-up to play. And I was out of practice being around people. But I didn't quit. I wrote. I learned. I made good friends. And along the way, I read *Mrs. Dalloway* for the first time.

My symptoms were never the same as those of Septimus Smith, nor anything like as severe. For one thing, I never hallucinated, and perhaps this is why, when I first read the book, I didn't experience a particular connection to him, beyond the universal connection we all must feel to someone so damaged by trauma and in so much pain.

Or maybe a bit of the self-protection that kept me from seeing the connection between my father's death and my restored capacity to function in the world also kept me from drawing any kind of line from so tortured and tragic a figure, even a fictional figure, to myself. Maybe I have a tendency to postpone certain insights until I can handle them.

Though arguably I am not always good at judging for how long to preserve a seemingly self-protective ignorance. Had I drawn a few more connections at seventeen, when my therapist asked me about my father, instead of denying any strong feelings toward him, who knows what unhappiness I might have skipped along the way. But we can only do what we can do—when we can do it.

It wasn't until I immersed myself in *Mrs. Dalloway* this past year that I at last made the connection between my agoraphobic years and some piece of what Septimus Smith experiences—so perhaps some piece of what Woolf too experienced: that warp toward the self, that hover of danger everywhere. The hopelessness of not experiencing the world as others do. And though I marvel at the high wire brilliance of Woolf's use of point of view, I didn't merely marvel at her skill, as this realization seeped through, or even at her deep compassion. I understood better what my own experience had been, and I felt grateful for that, and I felt less alone.

Which in the end is perhaps something like what I felt that night on the train, and why I have always remembered that moment, and surely why it has been so much on my mind these past several months, as I have read and read.

Four

OBSCURING THE JUGGERNAUT

A CONFESSION: I AM BORED to tears by the section of *Mrs. Dalloway* that involves her daughter Elizabeth riding a bus. Bored. To. Tears. I have been through it a gazillion times, because if you are going to write a book about a book you really are obligated to read the whole thing, and read it well. And then read it again. But it's a struggle every time. I am not interested in Elizabeth Dalloway. I am not convinced that she plays an important enough role in the scheme of the book to earn so many pages (I know, I know, it isn't really that many) nor do I think she informs us enough about women of her generation, or society, or her mother, or, honestly, anything.

Bored. To. Tears.

Maybe I am bored because Elizabeth Dalloway is boring:

> So she might be a doctor. She might be a farmer. Animals are often ill. She might own a thousand acres and have people under her. She would go and see them in their cottages. This was Somerset House. One might be a very good farmer . . .

Animals are often ill.

As even her mother knows, she is not brilliant. Clarissa notes "the tradition of public service in the Dalloway family" with the implication that Elizabeth might follow a long line of Dalloway women who served as "Abbesses, principals, headmasters, dignitaries . . . without being brilliant, any of them."

Possibly, I am also bored because there is no thread in this scene, nothing to follow, nothing unfolding—and I cannot hold onto the point of view. Is it a distant narrator? Are we entirely in Elizabeth's head? Does the girl who thinks, "animals are often ill" also think:

> Forgetfulness in people might wound, their ingratitude corrode, but this voice, pouring endlessly, year in year out, would take whatever it might be; this vow; this van; this life; this procession, would

> wrap them all about and carry them on, as in the rough stream of a glacier the ice holds a splinter of bone, a blue petal, some oak trees, and rolls them on.

I am certain there are readers and scholars out there who can explain why that syntax makes sense in this scene, but to me, as just one reader, what it looks like is that Woolf is struggling with this character and has made her a bit uninhabited, this ingenue with a conscience, and also that Woolf could not resist slipping some of her own wisdom in among young Elizabeth's thoughts, draped in the trappings of a narrator.

I don't find Elizabeth Dalloway to be a real character, not in the way Peter Walsh is, or even Richard Dalloway. Or even Hugh Whitbread. But of course you don't have to love every bit of a book to love the book. You don't have to think an author hits only home runs to think they are brilliant.

Though, in this case, I do think it's a bit more complicated than that.

A very wise teacher once told me that the greatest service a reader of a work in progress can perform is telling the author where the heat is in the piece, and where it seems to go cold.

Virginia Woolf isn't asking for my advice, and *Mrs. Dalloway* is not a work in progress, but I can't help but feel that this book, which is heated around so many subjects, from fear of death to joy in mending a torn dress, from collective grief to the pleasure of having an enemy, from the horrors of war to the horrors of care for the mentally ill, is stony cold on the subject of motherhood. It is that rarest of works of literature: a novel about a woman who is a mother that has absolutely no interest in being a novel about being a mother.

There are any number of possible reasons for this. Woolf, having lost her own mother at the age of thirteen and never having had children of her own may have found the subject painful; she may have found it tedious; she may simply have had a different project in mind with this book. But what interests me here isn't trying to figure out why Woolf shut the subject down in *Mrs. Dalloway*, nor even whether she did so intentionally, but rather how the book turns away from the subject again and again.

Because, this boring scene notwithstanding, I admire this feat. It's hard to place motherhood in a work of fiction, and not have it be central. It's hard to put a mother in a book and have people see her as so much else before they define her by this role. Because motherhood is a juggernaut.

And this is where I want to write all-caps and bold: **AND BECAUSE PEOPLE ARE CRAZY ON THE SUBJECT.**

They are.

It never occurred to me, as I penned my short stories, that I would be accused of writing "bad mothers." But when my collection, *If loved you, I would tell you this*, was published, I met numerous readers who objected to what they perceived as the coldness of the mothers I depicted.

"Your mothers are all so cold. I couldn't relate to them."

All?

I definitely hadn't intended my fictional mothers to *all* be anything. I had worked hard to make each of these women into an individual. I had thought about their respective interests, their obsessions, their foibles, their consciences, their appearances, their passions, their talents, their homes, their sexual selves, their preferences in food, their impulses, their tempers, their speech patterns, their drinking habits, and on and on and on. And I had also thought a lot about their respective relationships with their children, which varied from story to story—of course, since they were different women, with different children, in different situations. But what I hadn't thought about, not even a little bit, was whether they one and all violated some expectation of motherhood in a similar way, making them seem far more alike to some readers than I had anticipated, and making them all seem cold.

And they hadn't. I came to this conclusion after some serious consideration and multiple conversations in which I tried to drop my defensiveness and actually listen beyond the blare of that word "cold." There are ten stories in the book.[5] All of the stories include mothers in some role. Four are about women with active, even consuming concerns about a child who is not yet an adult. Three of the stories are about women in their sixties and seventies who have adult children. The rest are about mothers who are minor figures, some barely characterized at all.

Gradually, I realized that in spite of that word "all" the truly problematic mothers, the ones so often viewed as "cold," were the three older women with adult children. I had thought of their motherhood as a fact about these women, but not as the central fact and surely not as the subject of the story—much as I suspect Woolf viewed Clarissa's motherhood: a fact about her.

My seventy year old character Clara has adult children,

5. Eleven in the later paperback edition.

yes, but the story is about her grief over the loss of her lover and how that grief dovetails with her work as a portrait painter. Kate, a sixty-five-year-old woman, recently left by her husband of many years, also has adult children, but the story is about her relationship with her twin brother and the lasting impact of her guilt over neurological damage he sustained during their shared birth. Another story centers on Jean, a seventy-something woman who is dealing with her husband's impending death and with her own changing sense of self, readying herself for this goodbye, adjusting to a life without partnered sex.

These are women whose children are adults with families of their own. Their concerns are not centered on their grown children. Their days are not taken up with their grown children. And, as far as I understand, their "coldness" is evidenced by their seeing faults and irritating aspects to those grown children. Clara says something a bit sharp to her adult daughter in a very brief remembered scene. Kate has recently been left by her children's father and feels that they—and others—have not been enough on her side as her long marriage has crumbled. And Jean dislikes the way her kids think they know best how she should live her life, and finds her daughter a bit reckless—a quality that manifests in the story, proving her assessment to be correct.

So, what it comes down to is that in a book that depicts more than ten mothers, three mothers of adult children do not show enough wholly uncritical adoration for them. And these are not women who are wholly uncritical of anything. It isn't as though they have made some negative exception for how they view their own offspring. The problem turns out to be that they did not suspend their usual critical thinking skills when dealing with their kids.

And then, like some scene out of *Frozen*, their coldness expanded and overtook the other stories in my book, so that somehow, magically, "all" of my mothers became cold.

Because . . . PEOPLE ARE CRAZY ON THE SUBJECT.

They are.

But that isn't much of a stopping point, when it comes to understanding what, from my perspective, went wrong.[6]

To be a bit more analytical, there were two major issues, two glitches between my intentions for how these characters

6. To be clear, just as I defend my right to find Elizabeth Dalloway boring, I defend these readers' rights to find my mothers cold. That was not my intent, but as I have said before, and will say again, the thing about intent is that it isn't complete control. And for the purposes of literature, it shouldn't be.

would be received, and how, in too many cases, they were. The first was that in spite of my not having at all meant these women to be viewed primarily as mothers, they were. The second was that there was a leap made from the fact of their having a few complaints about their grown kids to their being cold, to their being "bad mothers."

Maybe that is two leaps, but they were in the same direction.

Another confession: When I first read *Mrs. Dalloway*, to the extent that I thought about this aspect at all, I thought Clarissa was a bad mother. I may even have found her cold.

There are some criticisms to be leveled. She entrusts her daughter to her "enemy," the unfortunate Miss Kilman, a woman she herself finds odious. She believes there is a romantic connection between this dank smelling, middle-aged woman whom she despises and her very young daughter, but . . . *c'est la vie*, this too shall pass.

In addition, Clarissa is throwing a party, *the* party, worrying through her own outfit, the flowers, the guest list, endlessly, but is not a bit concerned about her daughter's role or presentation or enjoyment—though in an odd conflation of this and the Miss Kilman business, we have this:

> With a sudden impulse, with a violent anguish, for this woman was taking her daughter from her, Clarissa leant over the bannisters and cried out, 'Remember the party! Remember our party tonight!'"

It is weak sauce if you truly believe someone horrible is taking your child from you, even emotionally. And the thought that Elizabeth might forget the party is indicative of how little involved she is in her mother's grand preoccupation.

Clarissa also dwells on her past a lot—a lot—but never muses on her daughter's birth or childhood. The signs of maternal attachment are scant. She thinks of Elizabeth during her walk in the opening scenes. A bit. She refers to her as "my Elizabeth"—a note that rings false to Peter Walsh, though I'm not holding him up as a judge of much when it comes to Clarissa. Or mothers. He seems a bit fixated on what he calls "the egotism of motherhood."

And so, having taken all that in, and probably a few more incidents and turns of phrase, I did what people do: I decided she was a bad mother. Or anyway, a cold and detached one. But I didn't think much of that. It wasn't the part of the book that interested me. It was a readerly aside, a feature of Clarissa I noted, low on the list.

And, unlike those readers of my own, I never found imperfect parenting to be unrelatable.

I became a mother at twenty-five—to a girl named Elizabeth. (I may as well add to my confessions here, that yes, my older daughter is called Elizabeth, and I have, not once but twice, married men named Richard.) I became a mother at what was in my circles a very young age, because I was afraid of the world, afraid to leave my house, and also because I had this idea that if I raised a child without the extreme challenges of my childhood, if I doted on her and built up her self-confidence and her self-esteem, the result would be two healthy individuals. I would fix myself, while not breaking her. On the morning after her late night birth, I woke and thought, "I am happy for the first time in my life. *This*, this new feeling I am having, is what happiness is."

And that was genuine, as it still is—happiness because of her, and because of her two younger siblings. Being a mother has brought me tremendous joy, a steady current running alongside all the challenges and usual frustrations and yes, the irritations one's children provide. Joy. But it wasn't only joy I was after, when I first set out. Motherhood was meant to save me—from the world, and from being myself. (Speaking of the egotism of motherhood . . .) Motherhood was supposed to usher in a peaceful, steady era in my life.

(Spoiler alert: It did not.)

Eight years later, I had three children, an ex-husband, and a new husband—who would try hard not to look annoyed when people called him Richard the Second. It probably goes without saying that the intervening time was not a peaceful, steady era of my life.

By then, I was years into being a stay-at-home mother, not because that was my dream occupation but because I was terrified of being out in the world. There were elements of being home with my kids that I absolutely loved. I have a strong domestic side. I love cooking, home design, gardening, and I pursued them all. I did endless art projects with my children. I enjoyed their company—most of the time, anyway (I mean, they were kids). And I did not resent them, which I say because as much as I enjoyed many aspects of those years, I did resent that I had planned a whole life around my fears.[7]

I also resented that when some people heard what my primary occupation was, they made shockingly condescending

7. Even with whatever resentments, I always appreciated the fact that I was able to make this choice. Only a degree of economic stability and privilege allowed for any of this.

(and shockingly clear) assumptions about me. I was less intelligent than I might have been were I in some profession, really any profession. I was unambitious—with all that implied. I might be creative, but not in any way that counted. Not in any way they could respect. (Cakes, Halloween costumes, paint-your-own pottery . . .) And children were my life, they assumed. I loved children, they assumed. I loved all children, everyone's children. I was the kind of woman who loved children, who finds them endlessly enchanting. And I was interested in *their* children. Maybe even more than they were. (I was not.) They were the first to admit that they would find being around children that much to be boring; they needed more intellectual stimulation. But I was a nurturing type, a real mom.

And when toward the end of this era of my life I started voicing an ambition to write, a truly bizarre number of the people to whom I confided that hope, asked if I would be writing children's books—not because I had ever expressed any interest in children's literature but because they literally could not imagine me doing anything that wasn't somehow connected to children.[8]

8. I have great respect for the writers and artists who create children's literature. I was just confused by the assumption that I was joining their ranks.

Like I said, motherhood is a juggernaut. And people are nuts.

When I first read *Mrs. Dalloway*, and faulted Clarissa for her mothering, I was seventeen years younger than I am now, and considerably younger than Clarissa Dalloway. My youngest child was eight years old, my oldest fifteen. I was in the thick of it, the subject of motherhood looming large for me.

I am no longer in the thick of it. And I no longer find it odd or indicative of a faulty maternal attachment that Clarissa thinks of her own youth, and not her seventeen year old daughter's infancy, or childhood—much less, birth. Nor do I think she should have chosen the day of her party to sort through the Miss Kilman thing. Nor am I surprised that she didn't much involve her seventeen year old daughter in her own party planning.

And far from wishing Clarissa were more besotted by her daughter, I would be put off were she to go on, as Richard Dalloway does,[9] about "adoring her Elizabeth." I

9. Woolf has a bit of fun with Richard's besotted heart when he doesn't recognize his daughter at the party. There's a hint of his not quite seeing her clearly for who she actually is, and also, I think, a nod to the fine line between fatherly adoration and the family of mistake made famous by Oedipus.

would question her sincerity and her motive—not because mothers don't adore their children, but because, except on rare occasions, I associate that kind of gushing with an early phase of motherhood. It's been a long time since I've heard any of my friends who are around my age, with kids around my own kids' ages, express themselves that way. They are far more likely to talk about what is happening with their children, the good news that bubbles up from the younger generation to our own, the challenges, the worries, the annoying bits, along with the fun parts. And that isn't being cold. It's moving on. Appropriately.

But the truth is that even when I read *Mrs. Dalloway* the first time, I knew better. I knew that motherhood comes in all forms, and that one needn't be evidently besotted or always get it right to be a fine mother. I even knew that the notion of the "bad mother" is a dangerous one, laden with a treacherous history of misogyny. I had fallen into this odd and fascinating trap of fiction: the emergence of default and questionable ideals.

It turns out that fiction lulls us away from our rational minds. But I knew that too, or I should have. We authors count on it, we acknowledge it when we speak hopefully of readers "falling into the dream." In order for fiction to work at all, it has to sidestep the rational brain. We all know perfectly well that it's entirely possible that Jane Austen's last page happy couples will grow sick of one another, irritated half the time, regretting their union. After all, we have the stats and we have life experience. It can happen to even the most rapturous of us. But we let ourselves believe, for that moment, that they won't. We do so with a kind of gratitude for a relief from the burden of reality.

And I have found that when it comes to mothers there is that dangerous and common default ideal, culturally determined and harmful, that can sneak out when some readers are in the dream state. When I first met Clarissa, I compared her to that ideal and found her wanting, failing to meet her on her own terms, failing to apply my knowledge that mothering takes and should take many forms.

Though, to be fair, if Clarissa were a personal friend, I would still absolutely suggest that she find a less problematic tutor for her child, one whom she herself doesn't think odious . . . but we are none of us perfect. Which is perhaps the point. We don't have to be. We can't be.

It isn't just readers for whom this ideal emerges. It is writers, as well. From time to time, when I teach, or read a friend's early draft manuscript, a woman will appear on the page who has no detectable identity beyond her near-obsessive adoration of her children. In one such instance, in a workshop, I asked the author if the woman depicted suffered from some kind of mental illness. The answer was no, accompanied by a puzzled, "Why?"

"Because she is so obsessed with her adult son that I thought she might be meant to be mentally ill."

I received significant pushback. A number of the workshop participants, for the most part in their twenties, claimed that it actually seemed like a pretty accurate representation to them. "You haven't met my mother!" more than one person said.

That was true. I had not met their mothers. But I have met a lot of mothers, hundreds if not thousands of them, some of whom are my very close friends; and I have never met one as uncritical of her own children, nor as intent on centering her life around them once they were adults. I have never met one who has no interests outside her children.

I pushed back on the pushback and asked if their mothers truly thought of nothing but their own children, and the eventual answer was, no, of course not. Every one of them had a job of some kind, every one of them had a social life. Many had a partner.

I wondered whether these writers, not so many years out from leaving home, needed to believe that their mothers were nonstop obsessed with them in order to feel comfortable about stepping away, but the fact is, I have seen this maternal figure in the work of writers far from that stage of life. I saw it in myself as a reader, when judging Clarissa Dalloway. To some number of us, that version of motherhood, idealized and unrealistic, problematic though we know it is, lurks just below the rational part of our minds that remembers about the jobs, friends, and hobbies, the part that knows how unhealthy such an identity would be.

It all plays on the same fantasy doesn't it? The fantasy of The Good Mother who sees us through a glass so thickened with rosy hues that it hides all our flaws. The Good Mother whose life offers no significant competition for the joy she might get from time in our company. The Good Mother whose life hit a high when the kids were her main concern and who cannot move past mourning that. The Good Mother whose love for us is not only unconditional, but uncritical, as well.

When I set out to write my novel *Life Drawing*, I knew

nothing about it, except that if there was to be a woman at its center, she would neither have nor be a mother. This was a rare decision for me, to form a character not from the needs of the story, but from my own. By then though, in both my daily life and my writerly life, I felt too defined by motherhood. I was, frankly, sick of the whole subject. (Though not of my own children nor of being their mother. The *experience* of motherhood is distinct from the *subject* of motherhood.) I had written a collection of short stories, not as an extension of my maternity, but as what felt like a huge step away from a life exclusively defined by that. Yet the reality of my having been a mother for my entire adult life permeated those pages. To many readers, fairly enough, that was what the book was about, and I wanted to move away from that categorization.

Moreover, the term "domestic fiction" was starting to have a kind of sickly sweet stench to it, at least when applied to fiction by women, and I hoped that perhaps by writing primarily about a woman who did not have children, I would somehow dodge that section of the bookstore.

In my personal life too, I was tired of people to whom I had not given birth viewing me as maternal. A published author, I was no longer subject to the offensive stereotypes that had trailed me through my years as a stay at home mom, but somehow motherhood still loomed large in my extra-domestic identity, in a way that saddened and frustrated me. Younger friends often told me I was like a mother to them, or a mother figure, or that they loved how maternal I was, and I felt, not honored as was intended, but negated by being so categorized, aged out of relevance as a friend, and also placed—unconsciously, I am sure—in an entirely uneven relationship. Whether rightly or wrongly, I heard more than a hint in this categorization that we, as a dyad, would be tended and tender; confider and advisor; needy and nurturer.

I needed a break from all of that. And so my novel's narrator Augusta (Gus) Edelman, late forties, no kids, mother dead since her toddlerhood, was born.

As if it were all as simple as that.

Yes, Gus, is both without a mother and without a child, but somehow, the novel is still about motherhood. In part, this is because Gus keenly misses having had a mother, and thinks about herself as "motherless," and about what that has meant in her life. And then, there is a major plot point that arises because of decisions a different character makes about her own daughter, decisions that grow out of an aspect of her mothering, a possibility that my narrator has not anticipated, in part because she has never experienced any kind of mother-child connection, so does not think in those terms.

If you make your central character obsessed with a subject, as I did with Gus and her longing for her deceased mother, you have made the subject central to the book. If you connect a subject to the causality of a major plot development, as I did, you have made it a central subject of the book.

I could strip my narrator of whatever familial connections I liked. I still wrote a book about motherhood.

But I tried not to, and in that effort, I feel a humble connection to Woolf, because I believe she tried hard not to make that a central subject of *Mrs. Dalloway*—and was more successful than I. In a sense she did the inverse of what I did (or visa versa). My narrator Gus was motherless and childless, but the subject found its way to the novel's center anyway. Clarissa (also motherless) has a daughter, her Elizabeth, yet the subject is systematically pushed to the periphery. Woolf may or may not have been interested in the subject of motherhood. Her novel *Mrs. Dalloway* is not.

Which brings me back to Elizabeth Dalloway noodling

away about her possible career paths while she rides that omnibus. I said that I don't find her a successful character in the way many others in the novel are, and I don't. But I'm not a bit sure that Woolf wanted us to experience her in the same way.

Elizabeth Dalloway seems to me to be something of an authorial obligation. She ticks a necessary box. It is necessary that Clarissa and Richard produced one child, and also that they produced only one. She is the procreative measure of their limited but not non-existent sex life. Clarissa isn't so "cold"—Woolf's word—that she and her husband never had any sex, but nor was she into it enough that, like that sexy lifeforce Sally Seton, she ended up with baby after baby after baby. Elizabeth Dalloway is necessary to tell us something about her mother—but not because Elizabeth Dalloway is, as Clarissa might say, this way or that, but because she exists. And because she is an only child[10].

---

10. We do not know the exact age at which Clarissa married Richard, but she was approximately thirty-four when she had Elizabeth. This gap of almost certainly more than a decade is a never acknowledged peculiarity. I suspect it is just an outgrowth of Woolf wanting both Clarissa and Elizabeth to be the ages they are at this time, but whatever its genesis, it means that Clarissa and Richard had many years together without a child, and also that motherhood came to Clarissa at what was, in the Edwardian

But it isn't only conveying a measure of her parents' sex life that necessitates Elizabeth's existence. For Clarissa not to be a mother would draw attention to the subject of motherhood. It would open up questions about her feelings on the presence of that absence, and about Richard's. It might add a poignancy to her wondering about her alternate reality as Peter's wife, this question of whether they might have had children. It would inevitably, given the era and the social world of the Dalloways, put the subject right at the center. And so, we must have Elizabeth Dalloway, not to enhance our thoughts about Clarissa's motherhood, but to set them aside.

I wouldn't say that with any confidence, were there not so many signs that this is Woolf's intent: to shut the subject down, starting with the two mothers mentioned early on who lost sons in the war. One might think their motherhood would be prominent in this mention of their loss, but in an odd way, it is not:

> The War was over, except for some one like Mrs. Foxcroft at the Embassy last night eating her heart out because that nice boy was killed and now the old Manor House must go to a cousin; or Lady

era, a very advanced age.

> Bexborough who opened a bazaar, they said, with the telegram in her hand, John, her favourite, killed; but it was over; thank Heaven—over.

Their sons are killed, but their grief is truncated, in Lady Bexborough's case by her duty at the bazaar, and in Mrs. Foxcroft's by the sleight of hand whereby that grief is now over a piece of property rather than a child. Far from being asked to imagine what it must be like to so grieve, as a mother, we are directed away from doing so. It is subtle, and, again, were it the only instance of a kind of swerve from the topic of motherhood, it might be meaningless, but it is far from the only example of our being asked, again, again, to turn our gaze away.

The number of women in the book who do not have children is notable Miss Kilman has no children. Miss Brush has no children. Ellie Henderson has no children. Aunt Helena Parry has no children.[11] Lady Bruton also seems to have no children, and in fact, with a sleek rhetorical move, Woolf uses her to discourage us once again from thinking

11. Of course, in post-World War One England, there was a dearth of men, and so many women who might otherwise have wanted to marry and have families (or who might have just done it because it was expected of them) could not, but the women listed here are primarily not of an age to be in that group.

in terms of maternity, as when she contemplates "her family, of military men, administrators, admirals, had been men of action, who had done their duty . . ." No women, no mothers, nobody but men in this family line.

Lucrezia wants a child but cannot conceive with a husband who will not have sex with her. Peter Walsh's paramour Daisy does have children, but their future together would involve her essentially dissolving her motherhood: "It was a question of her position, Mrs. Burgess said; the social barrier; giving up her children." In a sense, if she is to fulfill her role in this narrative, she too must become childless.

Sally Seton has children, five of them, but in an exchange with Peter Walsh, the notion of this being interesting is efficiently knocked down. She tells him she has five sons, he muses on the egotism of motherhood (he really is stuck on that) and a few exchanges later, he says of their fellow party guests, "Everyone here has six sons at Eton," making clear that Sally producing five sons is neither an accomplishment nor a matter of much interest.

It is a systematic minimizing of the subject, a gentle push of our attention, away.

And there are further instances, more directly related

to Clarissa herself. Many of the things I attributed to "bad mothering" when I first read the book, I now see as critical to this scheme of Woolf's. Clarissa does not think about Elizabeth in the context of the party, because Woolf doesn't want us thinking that anything about that event is motivated by hopes or plans or concerns about her daughter. Clarissa doesn't think about her daughter's childhood because Woolf wants us to draw a straight line between eighteen year old Clarissa Parry and the Mrs. Dalloway whom we meet, without interference.

There is one mention of Elizabeth's birth, in the passage where Clarissa muses on her own lack of sexual passion: "she could not dispel a virginity preserved through childbirth which clung to her like a sheet." The focus is on her sexual self, but Woolf needn't have brought childbirth into that. Like so many other passages in the book, this image pulls away from motherhood, as though the impact of childbirth has been somehow smoothed over in Clarissa. It would have been easy enough for Woolf to choose a different measure of Clarissa's persistently virginal state, but she chooses to negate the moment at which she becomes a mother. If Clarissa's virginity has somehow survived childbirth, then so, on some level, has her childlessness. But if it is a virgin birth, it is also an oddly inconsequential one, as Elizabeth is absent from so much of what consumes her mother:

> Did it matter then, she asked herself, walking towards Bond Street, did it matter that she must inevitably cease completely; all this must go on without her; did she resent it; or did it not become consoling to believe that death ended absolutely? but that somehow in the streets of London, on the ebb and flow of things, here, there, she survived, Peter survived, lived in each other . . .

When I first read this, I was struck by the fact that Clarissa imagines herself living on in Peter, and Peter in her, as opposed to her sharing that imagined eternity with her husband—and indeed that is both odd and pointed. But I realize now that these lines also entirely skirt the more common fantasy—or hope—that we live on in our children. Death is such an enormous preoccupation for Clarissa Dalloway. Her coping with the reality of mortality is central to this novel. Here, as we are first introduced to the subject, there is no mention of the role of having progeny in any potential "survival."

To the end, Clarissa fails to connect her own parenthood with her own central concerns:

> Then (she had felt it only this morning) there was the terror; the overwhelming incapacity, one's parents giving it into one's hands, this life, to be lived to the end, to be walked with serenely; there was in the depths of her heart an awful fear.

The use of "one" here may broaden the imagery to include all of humanity, but does not in any way address that she too has put another human being in this existential trap, which would be a enough natural thought to have.

This could all be put down solely to Clarissa's character, to Woolf wanting us to view Clarissa's motherhood as peculiarly detached, and I think there is an element of that. Clarissa is hard, Sally Seton tells us. She is cold, Clarissa tells us herself. But it is important to remember that these are decisions Woolf made. Woolf was not presented with a cold, hard Clarissa Dalloway, who has a detachment from motherhood; she invented her.

Woolf is also responsible for the fact that Elizabeth is

always described as related to her father's line—all those highly effectual Dalloway abbesses and headmistresses from whom she has gotten her lack of brilliance—and is never credited with any Parry in her. And then there is the passage in which Clarissa thinks about the fact that her daughter's looks are unexpected, "dark (with) Chinese eyes in a pale face" and speculates that perhaps this is the result of "the Dalloway ladies" perhaps "mixing" with foreigners at some point in history.

The language of this passage is offensive (one reason I am paraphrasing it) but, importantly, it expresses again this sense of Elizabeth not belonging to her mother, not only because her appearance is unexpected, as though she were some kind of changeling, but because, in Clarissa's thoughts, it is possible only that the unexpected traits came through the Dalloway line. It would have been easy enough for Woolf to write about Clarissa's confusion that Elizabeth doesn't resemble her at all, or that Elizabeth resembles neither of her parents, but Woolf instead writes Clarissa's role out of these conjectures —as is consistent with this novel's repeated request that we not think too much about motherhood.

Virginia Woolf lost her mother young, and had no children.

I am a sixty year old who speaks to my mother daily, and has three children who are very much a part of my life. Is this just a case of "write what you know?"

Maybe. Though by now I have come to see that it's not just what I know; I also find mothering and the subject of motherhood interesting. I may have had reasons, both social and professional, for wanting to step away from it in my non-familial identity and in my work, but I stepped back toward it in my novel not only because it is my area of expertise, but because in fact I like pondering this role, this relationship, in all its intricacy.

And to dismiss Woolf's systematic quashing of the subject by saying that as a woman without children she wrote what she knew, misses both the radical and the skilled nature of what she did. Radical, because in 1925 it was not so common to suggest that the most compelling aspects of a woman with a child might not be that at all, not even a little bit, that her motherhood is not centrally relevant to her identity.

And skilled because this is a tightrope she is walking; or perhaps she is engaging in sleight of hand, with all the elements of misdirection and distraction inherent to such tricks. Clarissa cannot *not* have children, because in her social world that would be too large and distracting a fact about her and motherhood. So she has one child. But she must almost never think about that child—just enough that this absence of thought is shy of pathological, barely noticeable. And Richard must fill in the emotional blanks here, so we aren't tempted to wonder about the cold home in which this child has been raised, but he mustn't think of their daughter so much that the contrast between him and Clarissa places too bright a light on her detached motherhood. And the supporting characters must conspire in directing us continually away from this subject. Clarissa's own mother must be dead, another muffling of motherhood, but Clarissa cannot dwell on that. Though it would, again, be too odd, if she absolutely never thought of her, so there are a couple of glancing references. And as for the child herself, she must exist, and must spend some time with Clarissa, because for that not to happen would be too strange, but she mustn't be so interesting that our focus drifts significantly to her.

It must be tempting to suggest that there are so many other enormous subjects in the novel that Woolf was precluded from centering motherhood as another. These include the aftermath of the War; matters of mental health;

worries about death; worries about romantic episodes long in the past. But the reality is that Woolf might have chosen to associate motherhood with any one of these. She could have taken a different angle on the women who lost sons in the war by perhaps having Clarissa think about what that would feel like, imagine herself losing Elizabeth. She might have given Lucrezia a child, which would have kept our eyes on the subject, highlighting Elizabeth through the parallelism of the story. She might have had Clarissa think of living on in her own child rather than in Peter; and she might well have connected Clarissa's memories of being eighteen to concerns or hopes or fears for her daughter who is now around that age. Had Woolf wanted to make Clarissa's motherhood central, and still address all of those other weighty topics, she could have. Love, illness, romance, every one of these has an inherent connection to one's thoughts and fears about one's children.

Woolf made an authorial decision to keep Clarissa's motherhood, and the subject of maternity in a larger sense, set aside, even severed, from these subjects. Yes, I thought about what kind of mother Clarissa is, all those years back when I first encountered her, but it was the passing thought of a reader who at the time saw the world very much through that lens. I'm not a bit sure that were I now to read the novel fresh, I would assess in her that context at all.

It turns out that it takes more than just giving a character a child or not doing so to determine whether motherhood, that juggernaut, grabs center stage.

What does *Mrs. Dalloway* tell us about motherhood?

Like the song says: *Absolutely nothing.*

What are we meant to think about Clarissa Dalloway as a mother?

It's a trick question: *We aren't.*

Not much, anyway.

As for my three older women characters who were deemed bad mothers, I suspect that had any of those stories been read outside the context of that collection, the subject might never have arisen. The book, overall, is about family life, with a heavy emphasis on parenting. It is possible that I primed my readers to look in that direction. It is even likely that I did, I now think, though a decade ago, new to publishing and quick to detect (and dislike)any static between my intent and a reader's interpretation, I couldn't see that fact. It is also possible that my deep connection to the subject, my interest in it, seeped into even those individual stories in ways I didn't intend, and still cannot perceive. Whatever the case, once readers defined those women by their motherhood, those readers were subject to all the same fantasies and ideals that so many of us bring to fiction; just as I was when I created them, Clara, Kate, and Jean, whether I knew it or not at the time.

And that we also bring to our lives. I now believe that the people who responded to my being at home with my children with a well-developed, pre-existing set of assumptions about me, essentially viewed me as a fictional character: The Stay-at-Home Mom. With my choice of occupation, I did the opposite of what Woolf does with Clarissa. I gave them too much information about my mothering, dizzied them with that, and unwittingly crossed a line into that fantasyland, the dream state that in certain contexts also has a role outside the page. After all, we don't only suspend disbelief for Jane Austen novels; we do it for the weddings we attend, as well. We know the stats, as I said. We all have our own experiences. But for that moment, we believe, and we are grateful for that relief from our own burdensome, all too depressing knowledge.

I used to feel nothing but anger at the people who treated me with such condescension, but now I get a little kick out of thinking that I, wildly imperfect person that I am, ambivalent full-time mother that I was, propelled them into the dream state without writing a word, providing them for just a moment with that figure of fantasy: The Perfect Mother.

Or anyway, I get a kick out of it until I remember how profoundly damaging that ideal has been to so many. Including me.

When my novel came out, I was again accused by a number of readers, of having written a "bad mother." Allison, the character who makes a fateful and thoughtless decision based on her relationship with her daughter was dinged for being too indulgent of that child, too blinded by her adoration of her girl.

"By the end, I really hated her. I couldn't relate to her at all."

And this is where I have to insert that shrug emoji my own children so often send:

¯_(ツ)_/¯

Because for all that we think we have a thing completely figured out, the odds are overwhelming that we do not—which is not such a bad thing, I believe.

Five

Dear Clarissa,

I hope I may call you that. I feel that I know you so well, it just comes naturally. You may call me Robin.

I have been thinking things through quite a bit, and by things I mean your life. I have a few pieces of advice. I know you consider Peter Walsh's letters to be "dry sticks," and I hope to do better than that. In fact, as long as his name has already come up, I may as well start with some words about old Peter.

Clarissa, it is time to set aside any thoughts that perhaps you should have married him. You were well out of that. And before you tell me that you know that, let me gently point out that you are still, regularly, thinking about what life might be like had you accepted him, and having to remind yourself, again, again, that you did the right thing. And honestly, after more than three decades, it is time to stop. I'm not saying you were necessarily right to marry Richard—I'll get to that—but for sure you were right not to marry Peter.

I know people like him. They are smart and they are exciting.

Even though they are also often morose, they are exciting—in part, because, as you sensed, they have no boundaries. And it can be unfortunately thrilling to feel oneself merge with another person, especially with one who has a bit of volatility to them. But I want you to think hard about the question of whether he is kind to you. Not adoring, not flattering, but kind. Because it seems to me that kindness is a necessary bar for a life partner to clear, and that anyone who is continually on about the defects of your soul does not clear that bar.

Mind you, I am not suggesting that your partner should be wholly uncritical; just not scathing. You may not have heard it when he thought to himself, or said to Sally, that you are arrogant, and unimaginative, and prudish, cold and hard, but surely you sensed the presence of those judgments. And he hurled plenty of barbs your way, like his calling you the perfect hostess when he knew that you were trying to be something else, cherishing your brown paper wrapped copy of William Morris, and reading Huxley, and yearning to be involved in the intellectual discussions of your time. He knew that would sting. And honestly, Clarissa, imagine what it would be like being married to someone apt to mutter "the death of her soul" over breakfast. Horrible.

The thing about people like Peter is that they are a mess. And for some of us—here I wholly identify with you—these people who are smart, who exhibit any form of adoration of us, who find their way past whatever scrappy boundaries we ourselves may have, can be strangely and dangerously attractive. I don't know how much you know about emotionally abusive relationships, but part of what happens is that by breaking you down with comments like that hostess quip, they then set you up to need to earn back their approval (any of this sounding familiar?) so there is something nearly irresistible about them.

A lot of this fell into place for me when Peter burst into tears in your drawing room on the day of your party. I have to be honest: The first time I learned that your reaction was that had you married him "all this gaiety" could have been yours, I thought the phrase was sarcastic. As in: Thank God I dodged this bullet. I had so much trouble believing that you meant it, that I ignored the stuff about your feeling extraordinary ease and light hearted.

But of course you did. You felt wonderful. You were comforting him, tending him, believing that you alone could make him all better. All of that feels so good, doesn't it? Especially with the threat of his lecturing you on the defects of your soul hanging over your head. (The defects of your soul, Clarissa! Come on.)

Besides which—and I tell you this because perhaps it will put a nail in the coffin of all this lingering doubt you have—your

Peter Walsh follows young women through London parks and streets. He is just that creepy. You probably imagined that he left your home and thought of nothing but how much he loves you still. But in fact he thought of how hard you have grown, and how sentimental. He mused on the false note you exhibited when introducing him to your daughter and hit a favorite theme of his, the egotism of motherhood—whatever the hell that means—and then he followed a very much younger woman and fantasized about her rosy lips.

Please, Clarissa, please do yourself a favor, and once and for all, set aside dreams of the daily gaiety of devoting yourself to soothing the fragile ego of a man who, though sometimes good company, is also a manipulative, emotionally abusive creep.

We all have them in our pasts. I have dated my share of nasty men who seemed like my soul mate for a time, who created an illogical desire, nay need, to make them love me—in spite of real cruelty on their part. I have been there, and have not forgotten the power of it all. But the difference between us is that I do not need to remind myself constantly how well out of it I am—because I have no doubts. And you need to reach that point of resolution.

I know this seems hard, and I understand that the way your life was set up, you had this one enormous decision to make, and you had to make it while still not much beyond childhood. It doubtless seems possible to you that you didn't make the right choice, though it's also possible you did; or you didn't; or you did. And the whole thing is just haunting, understandably.

I wonder if part of the problem isn't the fiction you read as a girl. Fiction has a way of fucking us up—with apologies for my language. (I will wait for you to recover.) In much of the fiction you doubtless read, the same fiction I read a century later (Jane Austen, the Brontes, and so on) the one we are destined for is so often the turbulent fellow, the man who begins the relationship by being mean to us, by being domineering. The "happy ending" is ending up with him. Let's face it, the nineteenth century novel in which the heroine ends up with lovely, ineffectual Richard Dalloway is wholly out of line with the norm. There would be no movies made.

We are trained to think it's the Peter Walsh fellow we're meant for. And it can be close to impossible to overcome that influence. (I wonder if any of this was lurking in your mind when the whole business of Richard being called "Wickham" came up, with its strong reminder of all things Jane Austen, and you got so irritated.) It can be hard not to hanker for some of that excitement, even when we know it comes accompanied by at least as much toxicity.

And to be clear, I am not saying that Richard was necessarily the right partner for you. Have you ever heard of the concept of a false polarity? Basically, it means that you are set up to believe you have a choice between two things (in this case people) and that framing of the choice causes you to shut down the part of your brain that seeks the actual best answer. My sense is that the pressures of Peter's proposal caused you to leap in Richard's direction as if he were your only other option, which he was not. And I am not necessarily talking about Sally Seton here, though I think it's time that I did.

Sigh.

I don't suppose you need a whole lecture on the strictures of society and the way they can deprive people of the ability even to know what they want, so let me just say this: When someone kisses you, and it is the most exquisite moment of your life, it doesn't necessarily mean you should spend the rest of your life with that person—a kiss is just a kiss, after all—but it does, perhaps, mean you should pay a bit more attention to the experience than you did, Clarissa. Or a different kind of attention. I understand that the societal taboo on choosing Sally must have made that a very complicated prospect, but I do wish you had forced yourself past your own discomforts, and past your comfort too—comfort with doing what is expected of you.

Again, I am not saying you should have immediately set up house with Sally. I am reminding you of something you already know, that through all those days when you were sorting through which man to marry—of the only two on the entire planet, it seems—you were in love with a woman. A woman, I might add, who had all the best qualities of both, and none of the pitfalls of either. Like Richard, and unlike Peter, she was lovely to you. Like Peter, and unlike Richard, she cared about ideas and shared books with you, and encouraged you to think. Her kiss excited you. Her presence in your home, under the same roof as you, elated you. When Peter interrupted the two of you, it felt as though you had hit your face on a granite wall in the dark. It felt shocking, and it felt bad. It felt like a reminder of what paths were open to you, and which was closed.

I'll be honest. The whole story of that summer at Bourton breaks my heart. But I understand you were in a complicated situation. A part of me wishes you could have run off with Sally—or better yet, stayed put with Sally, in your own life. But as I said (and as others have also said) a kiss is just a kiss, so I don't want to get carried away and assert that you should have spent your life with someone whose kiss excited you just because their kiss excited you. A lot of kisses are exciting, and it doesn't mean our fate is sealed.

But I wish you had paid better attention both to your response to a woman and to the other qualities Sally exhibited, all superior to those of your male suitors. There is game played nowadays called Kiss, Marry, Kill—sometimes with a cruder version of "kiss." The idea is that you must choose which one of those actions you would take toward each of three people. As I see it, you played an epic round of Kiss, Marry, Kill at Bourton that summer, kissing Sally, marrying Richard, and essentially killing Peter by turning him down—though I admit, he has stubborn zombie qualities. In doing so, you followed the pattern I have seen in nearly every round of this I have ever played. People "kiss" the one they find most attractive, marry the one they find nicest even if they don't find them super sexy, and kill off the one they like least—or the one who is simply left over.

What has always puzzled me about this approach is why they don't marry the one they find sexiest, as long as they also like them. It makes no sense, but given two choices, both of whom the player likes equally, they will generally choose to kiss the one they are most attracted to, and marry the one they are less attracted to, but whom they like well enough. And you too made this classic error. You should have kissed Richard, discovered how little it did for you, married Sally, the one you were in love with, and yes, killed Peter. You should absolutely have killed Peter.

Though, to be clear, I am not really saying you should have married Sally. I am not saying you should have married anyone.

What I really wish is that you had waited a bit and grown up some before making your choice—if such a choice had to be made. Maybe at eighteen, still under your stern father's roof, the idea of spending your life with a woman was unimaginable—it certainly seems as though you didn't imagine it. And perhaps it would have continued to be so all your life, which is sad, but I recognize that you were not raised to be a free spirit or rule breaker. But maybe, at a minimum, if a man it was to be, it might have been a man with some of Sally's kindness and Sally's intellectual interest, and her boldness, her lack of concern for what one is supposed to do.

I have always found it chilling that Peter knew just from seeing Richard that you would marry him. There's a lot about Peter to disparage, but he was smart enough to perceive that you were likely to marry someone who looked the part, who offered no controversy, and who raised no eyebrows. Richard was sent to you from Central Casting and he got the role.

But of course, that was all a very long time ago, and here we are. I hope at least that some of what I have said about Peter might help you stop wondering about life with him, but none of this addresses your life now, beyond that. And I do feel there are improvements to be made.

I am a bit older than you, Clarissa, but given the century between us, perhaps those years don't amount to much. We tend to live longer now—or anyway, we did, until we, like you, got hit by a pandemic and, perhaps unlike you, have handled it horribly. But that is another story for another letter.

I know you feel that you have become invisible. I feel that way too. Like you, I am post-menopausal, and I am experiencing what it means as a woman to lose the currency of youth in this society of ours, which is still shockingly like yours in many ways. It isn't great. There are women who say they welcome it, that they like being able to go under the radar. There are even cute memes (you'll have to look that one up) about how the great thing about being invisible is that you can do anything—you can be outrageous, you can raise hell without anyone seeing you. But that is not my experience. And I question the value of raising hell invisibly.

These days we have something we call "second acts." As I thought about your life, it came into my mind. I even scribbled "Clarissa Dalloway's Second Act," on the notepad by my bed. Because the notion that you might set out on some new endeavor kept nudging at me. I mean, parties are wonderful, I like throwing them, myself. But yours seem to be only an annual affair, so not an everyday occupation, and from what I can tell, the rest of your time doesn't appear to be taken up with anything that consumes you. So, I was thinking of things you might do—but I warn you, a lot of them require you to overcome that snobbery of yours. (This is what we call tough love. I have mixed feelings about it, but it seemed necessary right there.)

You might open a shop. My first thought was flowers, but that was just me being lazy. I met you when you were choosing flowers, so my mind went there. I actually think one of those shops where you sell fine furnishings and consult on home design might be just the thing. (I have thought of doing this myself.) Or, you could be an advisor to a catering firm. There must be so many people out there who also enjoy hosting parties but don't have your flair for getting all the details right. I am sure you would find plenty of work.

Or you could volunteer. Between the wounded veterans and the impoverished of London, there can't be any lack of need. And I don't mean, an hour here, an hour there. I mean, you could take on a cause. Look at Lady Bruton. I'm not sure her causes are such great ones, nor that she is particularly effective, but what she is, is engaged. She is engaged in the doings of her nation. And it is engagement, it is caring about something beyond oneself that can blunt the sting of the world's averted gaze as we age past what society finds most compelling about women.

And speaking of women, perhaps I have fallen into a trap myself, as I have suggested activities that are typical ones for women to pursue. Décor. Food. Volunteer work. Perhaps you should go learn about geology. Or enter politics. It's funny, you have a daughter who sees many paths for herself but lacks enough self-knowledge to favor any—which is understandable at her age. At that age, you exhibited just as little self-knowledge. (I had none.) But you are in your fifties now. You should know a bit more about what interests you—and you should do something about it.

Your Second Act is possible, Clarissa. Don't deprive yourself of it because of the same attachment to what people expect of you that led you not to let yourself think about your love for Sally, and that caused you to marry a kind man who looked the part but never lit your fire. You have given over enough of your life to what you are "supposed" to do and to be. It is time to move on.

And maybe to do so less alone? I couldn't help but notice that at your party there was no one there whom I would call a close friend. It seems to me that you have no confidantes. No BFF's with whom you can shoot the breeze. You must be so lonely, up there in your tower room, staring at your elderly neighbor as though she holds some secret key to the meaning of life, and contemplating the irrevocable nature of time. I would go mad. But it's easy enough to see why you are so alone. You hold yourself aloof. You are not an intimate sort. You surround yourself with formalities of one kind and another. I may fault Peter for hurling insults at you while expecting you to marry him, but I get the sense that some of what he hurls might stick. And as I am not proposing to you, but only proposing that you make the most of your life, I want to help you see that those qualities are not your friends. And you do need friends.

I suggest that you loosen up a bit, let down a few walls. Invite a woman acquaintance over and surprise her with a confidence. You could say, "I've lost all interest in sex, not that I ever had much. I was wondering if you've experienced anything similar." Or maybe not that. You could start small. You could say, "Do you ever feel like the world no longer sees you, now that you are past a certain age?" Or you could say, "I don't know if I ever told you that I had a sister who died when she was young. Her name was Sylvia. I don't speak of her much, but at times I wish I could." Or you could say, "Do you think it's wrong of me to employ a tutor for Elizabeth whom I consider to be my enemy?" Or you could simply say, "I feel like we never really talk about our lives. Not beyond the superficial details. How are you really doing?"

We are born alone, Clarissa, and we die alone. It is best that we not spend the intervening time in that state.

I realize that to care about others, to form close relationships is to make oneself vulnerable—and if I didn't know that from my own experience, I would surely know it from watching how the fact of Lady Bruton's luncheon snub decimated you. To recap, because I really do want you to think about how ridiculous this was: You learned that Richard was invited to a luncheon to which you were not invited and it made you think of death, your own death. You quoted poetry on the subject. You conjured images of feeling "shriveled, aged, breastless." Your brain and body seemed to be failing you.

It's a lot, Clarissa. With all respect in the world, I want to suggest that it is too much.

I too have had my feelings hurt when people prefer my husband to me. On one memorable occasion (that I wish I could forget) we walked into a dinner party smiling, arm in arm to a chorus of excited voices crowing, "There he is!" It stung. It did sting. It soured the entire night for me. But it didn't carry quite the existential angst wallop that Lady Bruton's snub seems to have carried for you. And honestly, I wish I could cure you of this "all interactions lead to death" mentality of yours. In part because, ouch! How awful to go through the world so quick to leap to the fact of one's mortality. I burned dinner: We're all going to die. My TV isn't working: We're all going to die.

But mostly, I want you to stop doing that because there are more constructive responses you might have. When those people cheered my husband's arrival and ignored mine, I did two things. I tried to think if I had offended them somehow, and then, since I couldn't think of any way I might have, I reminded myself that not everyone can love me or even much like me. And then I silently told them all to fuck off. That's three things, I guess. I did three things.

You won't be invited to everything. Not everyone will adore you. And yes, it can sting. But it shouldn't cause you to despair over your own mortality. That isn't even remotely helpful.

And as long as I am on the subject of women you know, the answer to the question of whether it's wrong for you to employ a woman you perceive as your enemy to be your daughter's tutor, is yes. Yes, it is wrong. It is obviously wrong. And it may be wrong for you to thus perceive her. What makes her your enemy?

I am sure there are those who think that her attraction to your daughter is bringing up your unresolved sexual feelings for Sally and so on and so forth, and that that is why you have her around, or why you hate her, or both, but I think that lets you off too easy. I think that is like when someone talks of nothing but themselves and people say, "It comes from insecurity." It sounds like a good theory, it is surely a generous one, but it's possible the person is just self-absorbed and thinks they are more interesting than everyone else. And it's possible you hate Doris Kilman because she does not fit your image of what women should be, or because she is of German descent, or because she smells bad. Or because she so clearly has contempt for you. Or maybe it truly is that her presence opens the wound of your unresolved sexual feelings for your friend. But whatever it is, she needs to go. Dismiss her, pay her a generous severance, and then, if you feel so compelled, try to figure out why you kept her around. You have put your daughter in an untenable situation stuck between the two of you, and you need to do better.

But enough scolding. I hope this has not come across as only that. I care about you, Clarissa. And in many ways, some of which surprise me, I identify with you. But as I said, I am older, and I should add, I have also had the benefit of good mental health care, which seems to be impossible for you—though I think it would be helpful if you could find some way to work through your grief over your sister's death, and the haunting sense you have that your marriage isn't all you might have wished it to be. And possibly a thousand other things. But my larger point is that

I have been able to learn some things about how to get through life as a highly emotional, overly sensitive, fearful person whose thoughts tend to drift to worst case scenarios. But who loves life—and who even loves throwing parties, and choosing the flowers herself. I have actually learned a lot, and I just wanted to share some of it with you. I wanted to try to be that friend you do not have, until a better option comes along.

Now get to work brainstorming what you want to do for a Second Act!

(And for God's sake fire Miss Kilman!)

Your friend,
Robin

ACKNOWLEDGMENTS

Many thanks, first to Curtis Smith for encouraging me, years ago, to be a part of Ig Publishing's *Bookmarked* series, and to Pamela Erens for more recently reminding me of how much I wanted to be, by sharing a draft of her wonderful book on *Middlemarch*. Thanks as well to Robert Lasner and Elizabeth Clementson of Ig, for allowing me to do this, and for their support. Gratitude as ever for my agent and friend Henry Dunow who is always there, always wise, and always makes me laugh—which matters in an agent, though nobody ever tells you that.

Perpetual thanks to my many teachers whose voices have been in my head—in a good way—through this process. Karen Brennan conducted the class I took for which I first read *Mrs. Dalloway*, when in graduate school, and I am grateful to her for the excellence of that experience. In a single workshop session, David Haynes taught me how clocks work in fiction, one of the most important craft lessons I ever learned, and one on which I lean heavily, here. And, as always, thanks to Steven Schwartz, mentor and friend, brilliant writer, and quite simply the best teacher there is.

The Rosenbach Library, in Philadelphia, allowed me to teach a class on *Mrs. Dalloway* several years ago, which reignited my fascination with the book, for which I am grateful—as I am to my students there, and to all my students, who teach me more about reading and about writing than they can imagine; and about far more than that.

My mother, Barbara Aronstein Black, remains one of my sharpest, smartest, most demanding readers, and this time around, she met her match in Ann Packer who has been equally insightful, generous of her time, and supportive. I cannot express how much it has meant, and how important it has been to have the ongoing help of these two brilliant women. My thanks and my love to you both.

My dear friends, Jane Cutler, Julie Stern, and Bonnie West, the people with whom I communicate pretty much daily, kept me going and kept me laughing through the pandemic, which for me will always also be my *Mrs. Dalloway* era. Writers all, they were invaluable resources as I struggled to focus and to push forward against the distractions and the worries and the fears of this harsh and dizzying world of ours. Special thanks to another writer and dear friend, Catherine Brown, for the joy of our long conversations, and for her hearing me out and helping me out, as I rehearsed possible chapter focuses and potential approaches to *Mrs. D.* Robert Thomas, poet extraordinaire, came through with some critically important and characteristically insightful feedback at a crucial moment. I feel daily how very lucky I am to have such smart and supportive friends.

My children who live afar, Elizabeth and Court, David and Jenn, thank you for always asking how it was going; never asking much more when the answer was a growl; and celebrating when the answer was finally, "It's going great!" I love you all.

As for Annie, the daughter who lived this book daily, lived my moods, and lived my disappearing to write (when you *definitely* needed me to help with Logan, the naughty Havanese Pandemic Puppy) you are always my support, my inspiration, and my joy. Thank you for everything you do—for us all—and especially for knowing when what I needed most was a visit from you and Logan, out in my studio.

As ever, I couldn't do much at all without all my husband Richard does and is. As kind as Richard Dalloway, as exciting as Sally Seton, and not a bit like Peter Walsh, he is the perfect partner. I am so, so fortunate.

OTHER BOOKMARKED TITLES

Mario Puzo's *The Godfather*
by Atar Hadari (forthcoming)

Mary Gaitskill's *Bad Behavior*
by JoAnna Novak (forthcoming)

Middlemarch and the Imperfect Life
by Pamela Erens

James Baldwin's *Another Country*
by Kim McLarin

Truman Capote's *In Cold Blood*
by Justin St. Germain

Vladimir Nabokov's *Speak, Memory*
by Sven Birkerts

William Stoner and the Battle for the Inner Life
by Steve Almond

Stephen King's "The Body"
by Aaron Burch

Raymond Carver's *What We Talk About When We Talk About Love*
by Brian Evenson

(For a complete series list, go to
https://www.igpub.com/category/titles/bookmarked/)